BURIED CAESARS

BURIED CAESARS

Essays in Literary Appreciation

BY

VINCENT STARRETT

I sometimes think that never blows so red
The Rose as where some buried Caesar bled.
　　　　　　　　—EDWARD FITZGERALD

CHICAGO
COVICI-MCGEE CO.
1923

FROM THE PRESS OF
E. W. STEPHENS COMPANY
COLUMBIA MISSOURI

FOREWORD

NOT long ago, in England, young writers were tagged with the names of their discoverers, or of the alleged founders of the "schools" to which, it was supposed, they belonged. Thus, in the "glorious nineties," one who was not of the "decadent" group headed by Beardsley and god-fathered by Wilde, was likely to be one of the pugilistic school principaled by Henley, and such an one was dubbed "one of Mr. Henley's young men." The practice feebly survives, and is not without its usefulness, since, in a tight corner, the youngster may seek refuge under the coat-tails of his master, who stoically must receive the blows intended for his *protegé,* and who undoubtedly is held responsible for sins actually not in his calendar.

I have no wish to hide behind a greater name, and what blows may be directed my way I shall not attempt to deflect to other shoulders; but I am genuinely eager to associate my name with that of the man whom I have delighted to call Master, and whose kindly encouragement and active support enabled me to enter a field already vastly overcrowded. . .

William Marion Reedy.

vii

Something perhaps like what I have suggested in my first paragraph, Mr. Reedy might have written, here, had he lived. He had promised to introduce my book. My own note must be a poor substitute.

I am, then, frankly "one of Mr. Reedy's young men." I belong to the "Reedy school of criticism," which, if often it stresses the perpendicular pronoun, or seems oracular, does so in all sincerity, with considerable gusto, and for the benefit not so much of established reputations as for reputations either yet to be made or that have suffered from neglect. I have only small respect for criticism as it is generally practiced, and make no pretence of being a critic in any official sense. It is to be noted that the essays which follow are essays in literary *appreciation.*

If often I have talked in capitals, it has been because I have felt keenly the injustice done distinguished men and important work by the silence which preceded my shouting—a silence which, save for my own clamor, in a number of instances, it must be admitted, has continued unbroken. In other instances, however, I am happy to know, my shoutings have served to call to the admiring attention of others in number, books and writers of high significance. And if such a statement seem to lack plausibility in the light of

any present renown of certain of the writers presented, it may be recalled that most of the papers
in this volume date back a number of years. . .
Not all the subjects, perhaps, fall into the groups
I have suggested in this and another paragraph,
but in each essay will be found its *raison d'être*.

VINCENT STARRETT.

CONTENTS

ARTHUR MACHEN
A NOVELIST OF ECSTASY AND SIN

OF SIN

SOME thirty-odd years ago a young man of twenty-two, the son of a Welsh clergyman, fresh from school and with his head full of a curiously occult mediaevalism, privately acquired from yellowed palimpsests and dog-eared volumes of black letter, wrote a classic. More, he had it published. Only one review copy was sent out; that was to *Le Livre,* of Paris. It fell into the hands of Octave Uzanne, who instantly ordered Rabelais and Boccaccio to "shove over" on the immortal seats and make room by their side for the author. The book was "The Chronicle of Clemendy"; the author, Arthur Machen.

A few years ago, not long after the great war first shook the world, a London evening newspaper inconspicuously published a purely fictional account of a supposed incident of the British retreat from Mons. It described the miraculous intervention of the English archers of Agincourt at a time when the British were sorely pressed by the German hordes. Immediately churchmen, spiritualists, and a host of others, seized upon it

1

as an authentic record and the miracle as an omen.
In the hysteria that followed, Arthur Machen, its
author, found himself a talked-of man, because
he wrote to the papers denying that the narrative
was factual. Later, when his little volume, "The
Bowmen and Other Legends of the War," appeared in print, it met with an extraordinary and
rather impertinent success.

But what had Machen been doing all those
long years between 1885 and 1914?

In a day of haphazard fiction and rodomon-
tade criticism, the advent of a master workman
is likely to be unheralded, if, indeed, he is fortunate enough to find a publisher to put him
between covers. Mr. Machen is not a newcomer,
however, as we have seen. For thirty years he has
been writing English prose, a period ample for the
making of a dozen reputations of the ordinary
kind, and in that time he has produced just ten
books. In thirty years Rupert Hughes and Rex
Beach will have written one-hundred-and-ten
books and sold the moving picture rights of all.

Of course, it is exactly because he does not
write books of the ordinary kind that Arthur
Machen's reputation as a writer was not made
long ago. His apotheosis will begin after his
death. The insectial fame of the "popular" novelist is immediate; it is born at dawn and dies

at sunset. The enduring fame of the artist too often is born at sunset, but it is immortal.

More than Hawthorne or Tolstoy, Machen is a novelist of the soul. He writes of a strange borderland, lying somewhere between Dreams and Death, peopled with shades, beings, spirits, ghosts, men, women, souls—what shall we call them?—the very notion of whom vaguely stops just short of thought. He writes of the life Satyr-ic. For him Pan is not dead; the great god's votaries still whirl through woodland windings to the mad pipe that was Syrinx, and carouse fiercely in enchanted forest grottoes (hidden somewhere, perhaps, in the fourth dimension!). His meddling with the crucibles of science is appalling in its daring, its magnificence, and its horror. Even the greater works of fictional psychology—"Dr. Jekyll and Mr. Hyde," if you like—shrink before his astounding inferences and suggestions.

It is his theory that the fearful and shocking rites of the Bacchic cultus survive in this disillusioned age; that Panic lechery and wickedness did not cease with the Agony, as Mrs. Browning and others would have us believe.

Of Hawthorne, Arthur Symons wrote: "He is haunted by what is obscure, dangerous, and on the confines of good and evil." Machen crosses

those perilous frontiers. He all but lifts the veil;
himself, indeed, passes beyond it. But the cur-
tain drops behind him and we, hesitating to follow, but dimly see the phantasmagoria beyond;
the ecstasies of vague shapes with a shining about
them, on the one hand; on the other the writhings
of animate gargoyles. And we experience, I
think, a distinct sense of gratitude toward this
terrible guide for that we are permitted no closer
view of the mysteries that seem to him so clear.

We glimpse his secrets in transfiguring flashes
from afar, as Launcelot viewed the San Graal,
and, like that tarnished knight, we quest vainly
a tangible solution, half in apprehension, always
in glamor. But it is like Galahad we must seek
the eternal mysteries that obsess Arthur Machen.
There is no solution but in absolution, for it is
the mysteries of life and death of which he writes,
and of life-in-death and death-in-life. This with
particular reference to Machen's two most important books, "The House of Souls" and "The
Hill of Dreams," in which he reaches his greatest
stature as a novelist of the soul.

There are those who will call him a novelist
of Sin, quibbling about a definition. With these
I have no quarrel; the characterizations are
synonymous. His books exhale all evil and all
corruption; yet they are as pure as the fabled

waters of that crystal spring. De Leon sought.
They are pervaded by an ever-present, intoxicat
ing sense of sin, ravishingly beautiful, furiously
Pagan, frantically lovely; but Machen is a finer
and truer mystic than the two-penny occultists
who guide modern spiritualistic thought. If we
are to subscribe to his curious philosophy, to be
discussed later, we must believe that there is no
paradox in this.

But something of what we are getting at is
explained in his own pages, in this opening paragraph from his story, "The White People," in
"The House of Souls": " 'Sorcery and sanctity,'
said Ambrose, 'these are the only realities. Each
is an ecstasy, a withdrawal from the common
life.' " And, a little later, in this: " 'There is
something profoundly unnatural about sin . . .
the essence of which really is in the taking of
heaven by storm.' "

Nothing, it may be supposed, is more completely misunderstood than sin; but from the
general vagueness on the subject one gathers that
it is unpopular. To be sure, there are innumerable catalogued sins of varying degrees of wickedness, a chromatic scale, as it were, fixed by the
state and by the church, and the sins of one are
not always the sins of the other. There are new
sins and advanced sins and higher sins, all in-

tensely interesting and not a little puzzling to the
lay mind, since they are neither new, advanced
and high, nor particularly sinful. The sin with
which Arthur Machen is concerned is an offense
against the nature of things, it has to do with evil
in the soul, and has little or nothing to do with
the sins of the statute book. This Ambrose,
whom I have quoted, would tell you that sin is
conceivable in the talking of animals; if a tree
were to wish you "Good morning," that would be
sinful, or if a chimney-pot were to leap down and
accompany you upon a walking-tour.

To quote: "What would your feelings be,
seriously, if your cat or dog began to talk to you,
and to dispute with you in human accents? You
would be overwhelmed with horror. I am sure
of it. And if the roses in your garden sang a
weird song, you would go mad. And suppose
the stones in the road began to swell and grow
before your eyes, and if the pebble that you no-
ticed at night had shot out stony blossoms in the
morning?"

Our misconception of sin, thinks Ambrose,
arises in large part from our looking at the matter through social spectacles . . . The average murderer, *qua* murderer, is not a sinner in the
true sense of the word; rather, he is a tiger. He
murders not from positive qualities but from neg-

ative ones; he lacks something which non-murderers possess. "Evil, of course, is wholly positive—only it is on the wrong side. . . . Sin in its proper sense is very rare; it is probable that there have been far fewer sinners than saints . . . It is harder to be a great sinner than a great saint . . . We over-rate evil, and we under-rate it. We attach such an enormous importance to the 'sin' of meddling with our pockets (and our wives) that we have quite forgotten the awfulness of real sin." And so on.

Sin then is, simply, "an attempt to penetrate into another and higher sphere in a forbidden manner . . . Holiness requires almost as great an effort; but holiness works on lines that *were* natural once; it is an effort to recover the ecstasy that was before the Fall. But sin is an effort to gain the ecstasy and the knowledge that pertain alone to angels, and in making this effort man becomes a demon." Obviously, this is not the sin of the legal code.

Ambrose I conceive to be Arthur Machen. There are only two realities; sorcery and sanctity —sin and sainthood—and each is an ecstasy. Arthur Machen's is a curious blend of both.

One of his most remarkable stories—certainly, I think, his most terrible story—is "The Great God Pan," at first published separately with

"The Inmost Light;" now included in "The House of Souls." It is the story of a surgical experiment upon a girl, as a result of which, for a moment, she is permitted a sight of the Great God, beyond the veil, with shocking consequences. Yet it is told with exquisite reticence and grace, and with a plausibility that is as extraordinary as it is immoral. Here is the conclusion of that story:

> What I said Mary would see, she saw, but I forgot that no human eyes could look on such a vision with impunity. And I forgot, as I have just said, that when the house of life is thus thrown open, there may enter in that for which we have no name, and human flesh may becomes the veil of a horror one dare not express. . . The blackened face, the hideous form upon the bed, changing and melting before your eyes from woman to man, from man to beast, and from beast to worse than beast, all the strange horror that you witnessed, surprises me but little. What you say the doctor you sent for saw and shuddered at, I noticed long ago; I knew what I had done the moment the child was born, and when it was five years old I surprised it, not once or twice, but several times, with a playmate, you may guess of what kind. . . And now Helen is with her companions."

There is the very quintessence of horror in the restrained suggestion of such passages. As for "The Hill of Dreams," I have found its reading one of the most desolate and appalling experiences in literature. Reading it, himself, years after publication, its author decided that it was a "depressing book." That is undoubtedly true, but spiritually as well as technically it marks, to date, the topmost pinnacle of his tormented genius. It reaches heights so rarefied that breathing is painful. To the casual reader this sounds absurd; hyperbolical if not hypocritical rant; but in a day when a majority of critics find it difficult to restrain themselves in speaking of James Oliver Curwood and place Jeffery Farnol beside Fielding and Stevenson, one can not go far wrong is indulging a few enthusiasms for so genuine an artist as Arthur Machen.

Of the reviewers into whose hands fell this remarkable book, in the year of its publication, 1907, only one appears to have valued it at its real worth—the editor of *The Academy* who, carried away by the tale and its telling, turned out a bit of critical prose which might have been lifted from the book itself. "There is something sinister in the beauty of Mr. Machen's book," he wrote. "It is like some strangely shaped orchid, the colour of which is fierce and terrible, and its perfume is haunting to suffocation by reason of its intolerable sweetness. The cruelty of the book is more savage than any of the cruelty which the book describes. Lucian shuddered at the boys who were deliberately

hanging an ungainly puppy; he had thrashed the
little ruffian who kicked the sick cat, before he
wrapped himself away from the contact of such
infamy in the shelter of his own imaginings.
For in 'The Hill of Dreams' you seem to be
shown a lovely, sensitive boy who has fashioned
himself a white palace of beauty in his own mind.
He has had time only to realize its full beauty
when disease lays it cold touch upon him, and
gathers him into her grasp, until he lies decaying
and horrible, seeing his own decay and seeing
that his decay makes the white palace foul. The
boys did not chant songs as they looped the string
round the neck of the uncouth puppy. Mr.
Machen fashions prose out of the writhings of
Lucian, who is dear to him: and his prose has
the rhythmic beat of some dreadful Oriental instrument, insistent, monotonous, haunting; and
still the soft tone of one careful flute sounds on,
and keeps the nerves alive to the slow and growing pain of the rhythmic beat. Lucian in ecstacy
of worship for the young girl whose lips have
given him a new life, pressed his body against
sharp thorns until the white flesh of his body was
red with drops of blood. That, too, is the spirit
of the book. It is like some dreadful liturgy of
self-inflicted pain, set to measured music: and
the cadence of that music becomes intolerable by

its suave phrasing and perfect modulation. The last long chapter with its recurring themes is a masterpiece of prose' and in its way unique."

After that, there would seem to be no need for further comment on "The Hill of Dreams." But there is!

This great novel perhaps is Machen's masterpiece, a circumstantial narrative of martyrdom, told by a master of style. The background of the book is as rich and complicated as the bewildered mind of him who reads it—varying with that mind in some odd way; an accurate account of the transfiguration of a highly imaginative boy before the world has dulled and corrupted him. The story loses a certain health in the telling, however. A fastidious nature is stronger, more coherent, more organized, than one that is unfastidious, because it is selective, and because it rejects rather than permits itself to be rejected. Machen permits Lucian Taylor to be rejected, and on this account the boy often appears to be without the energy of passion, and becomes what we call decadent, although by nature he is intensely human and normal; for it is human to feel that sunsets are more than sunsets, and that girls are more than girls.

There is an extraordinary incident of Lucian's basking in the heat of an intolerable hour, an hour like the matrix of summer passion, in which much is intimated and little is told; yet one is half persuaded one has oneself experienced it. Indeed, throughout the whole telling, one writhes as at the tormenting memory of old dreams and emotions.

"The Hill of Dreams" is a study in the morbid; not that it is morbid to be a flagellant, for in the world of the soul, as someone has said, there is neither health nor disease; the lad Lucian Taylor performs his rites from an aesthetic necessity. He makes his body bleed not to kill his desire for Woman, but rather to glorify her fittingly. He is not disclosed, of course, in a world too credulously to be regarded as truthful; it is too solitary.

One's single objection to the story is its dearth of wit and humor, a deficiency that leaves the air oppressive at times. This is too bad, for with a greater alertness in this department it might even have got home to the "owls and cuckoos, asses, apes and dogs."

In this novel, as in most of his writings, Machen is deeply concerned with the hidden mysteries of nature. The *occult* in clouds, in trees, in water, in fields and valleys, is for Arthur Machen the background of all mystery. I think he *fears* Nature.

Clouds perhaps are the element of landscape most rarely described, yet that which contains more than any other feature of natural phenomena the cheering or the sinister. Vapor commands an infinite variety of form, from the uprearing crystal mountain to the grotesque and impossible shape of evil. Its range of color is incredible—from dazzling white or the delicate tints of dawn and sunset to the forbidding storm-blackness or the terrifying hue of slaughter. Both form and color may change in an instant over the widest areas the eye searches, and every change is registered in rivers and lakes and earth vegetation.

In his peculiar way, Machen has felt this; herein, in large measure, lies the secret of his power . . . "The river wound, snake-like, about the town, swimming to the flood and glowing in its still pools like molten brass. And . . . the water mirrored the after glow and sent ripples and gouts of blood against the shuddering reeds . . ." Again, "He saw the steep slopes surging from the valley, and the black crown of the oaks set against the flaming sky, against a blaze and glow of light as if great furnace doors were opened. He saw the fire as it were smitten about the bastions, about the heaped mounds that guarded the fort, and the crooked evil boughs seemed to writhe in the blast of the flame that beat from heaven."

That is hot and romantic, and seems a complete statement, yet it is invested with a curious, almost tantalizing reticence. It is by this reticence, too, that Machen makes for magic; and the disquieting conviction that he is withholding strange and sinister and beautiful revelations becomes more pronounced as he carries the effect farther, and into the human relationships of the "Garden of Avallaunius" . . . "They spoke amongst themselves in a rich jargon of coloured words, full of hidden meanings and the sense of matters unintelligible to the uninitiated, alluding to what was concealed beneath roses, and calling each other by strange names." And again, "He heard the history of the woman who fell in love with her slave-boy, and tempted him for three years in vain . . . and at last in incredible shape won the victory."

Only in the garden of Avallaunius, said Lucian, is the true and exquisite science to be found!

OF ECSTASY

Quite as important as what Arthur Machen says in his manner of saying it. He possesses an English prose method which in its mystical suggestion and beauty is unlike any other I have encountered. There is ecstasy in his pages. Jo-ris-Karl Huysmans, in a thoroughly good trans-lation, perhaps remotely suggests Machen; both are debtors to Baudelaire.

The "ecstasy" one finds in Machen's work (of which more shortly) is due in no small degree to his beautiful English "style"—an abominable word which it is difficult, however, to avoid. But Machen is no mere word-juggler. His vocabu-lary, while astonishing and extensive, is not af-fected. His sentences move to sonorous, half-submerged rhythms, swooning with pagan color and redolent of sacerdotal incense. The secret of this graceful English method is a noteworthy gift for selection and arrangement. A passage from "The Hill of Dreams" is apropos:

Language, he understood, was chiefly important for the beauty of its sounds, by its possession of words resonant, glorious to the ear, by its capacity, when exquisitely arranged, of suggesting wonderful and in-definable impressions, perhaps more ravishing and fur-ther removed from the domain of strict thought than the impressions excited by music itself. Here lay hidden the secret of suggestion, the art of causing sensation by the use of words . . .

To win the secret of words, to make a phrase that would murmur of summer and the bee, to summon the wind into a sentence, to conjure the odour of the night into the surge and fall and harmony of a line; this was the tale of the long evenings, of the candle flame white upon the paper and the eager pen.

Nowhere better has it been expressed. He defines his method and exhibits its results at the same time. And dipping almost at random into the same volume, here is a further example of the method:

Slowly and timidly he began to untie his boots, fumbling with the laces, and glancing all the while on every side at the ugly, misshapen trees that hedged the lawn. Not a branch was straight, not one was free, but all were interlaced and grew one about another; and just above the ground, where the cankered stems joined the protuberant roots, there were forms that imitated the human shape, and faces and twining limbs that amazed him. Green mosses were hair, and tresses were stark in grey lichen; a twisted root swelled into a limb; in the hollows of the rooted bark he saw the masks of men. . . As he gazed across the turf and into the thicket, the sunshine seemed really to become green, and the contrast between the bright glow poured on the lawn and the black shadows of the brake made an odd flickering light in which all the grotesque postures of stem and root began to stir; the wood was alive. The turf beneath him heaved and sunk as with the deep swell of the sea. . .

And:

"He could imagine a man who was able to live on one sense while he pleased; to whom, for example, every impression of touch, taste, hearing, or seeing should be translated into odor; who at the desired kiss should be ravished with the scent of dark violets, to whom music should be the perfume of a rose garden at dawn.

This is not prose at all, but poetry, and poetry of a high order. And it is from such exquisite manipulation of words, phrases and rhythms that Machen attains his most clairvoyant and arresting effects in the realms of horror and dread and terror and beauty; from the strange gesturings of trees, the glow of furnace-like clouds, the somber beauty of brooding fields and too-still valleys, the mystery of lovely women, and all the terror of life and nature seen with the understanding eye.

The peculiar philosophy of Arthur Machen is set forth in "Hieroglyphics" and in "Dr. Stiggins: His Views and Principles." The first chapter of the latter work is a scathing satire on certain foibles and idiosyncracies of the American people—such as lynching, vote-buying, and food-adulteration—but as it is, on the whole, a polemical volume which, by the nature of the subjects it treats, can have less permanent interest than the author's other work, it needs less discussion; although as a specimen of Machen's impeccable prose it may not be ignored.

In "Hieroglyphics" he returns to those ecstasies mentioned in "The White People" and gives us further definitions. The word *ecstasy* is merely a symbol; it has many synonyms. It means rapture, adoration, a withdrawal from common

life, the "other things" . . . "Who can furnish a precise definition of the indefinable? They
(the 'other things') are sometimes in the song of
a bird, sometimes in the whirl of a London street,
sometimes hidden under a great, lonely hill. Some
of us seek them with most hope and the fullest
assurance in the sacring of the mass, others receive tidings through the sound of music, in the
color of a picture, in the shining form of a statue,
in the meditation of eternal truth."

"Hieroglyphics" is Arthur Machen's theory of
literature and life, brilliantly exposited by that
"cyclical mode of discoursing" that was affected
by Coleridge. In it he suggests the admirable doctrine of James Branch Cabell that fine literature
must be, in effect, an allegory and not the careful
history of particular persons. He seeks a mark
of division which is to separate fine literature
from mere literature, and finds the solution in
the one word *ecstasy* (or, if you prefer, beauty,
wonder, awe, mystery, sense of the unknown,
desire for the unknown), with this conclusion:
"If ecstasy be present, then I say there is fine
literature, if it be absent, then, in spite of all the
cleverness, all the talents, all the workmanship
and observation and dexterity you may show me,
then, I think, we have a product (possibly a very
interesting one) which is not fine literature."

Following this reasoning, by an astonishing sequence of arguments, he proceeds to the bold experiment of proving "Pickwick" possessed of ecstasy, and "Vanity Fair" lacking it. The case is an extreme one, he admits, deliberately chosen to expound his theory to the nth degree. The analytical key to the test is found in the differentiation between art and artifice, a nice problem in such extreme instances as Poe's "Dupin" stories and Stevenson's "Dr. Jekyll and Mr. Hyde," as Machen points out. By this ingenious method the "Odyssey," "Oedipus," "Morte D'-Arthur," "Kubla Khan," "Don Quixote," and "Rabelais" immediately are proven fine literature; a host of other esteemed works merely, if you like, good literature.

"Pantagruel" by a more delicate application of the test becomes a finer work than "Don Quixote," and in the exposition of this dictum we come upon one of the mountain peaks of Machen's amazing philosophy.

He begins the discussion with a jest about the enormous capacity for strong drink exhibited by *Mr. Pickwick* and his friends, and reminds us that it was the god of wine in whose honor Sophocles wrote his dramas and choral songs, who was worshipped and invoked at the Dionysiaca; and that all the drama arose from the celebration of

the Bacchic mysteries. He goes on to "Gargan-
tua" and "Pantagruel," which reek of wine as
Dickens does of brandy and water.

The Rabelaisian history begins: *"Grandgou-
sier estoit bon raillard en son temps, aimant a
boire net,"* and ends with the Oracle of the Holy
Bottle, *"Trinch . . . un mot panomphée,
celebré et entendu de toutes nations, et nous sig-
nifie, beuvez."* "And I refer you," continues
Machen, "to the allocution of Bacbuc, the pries-
tess of the Bottle at large. 'By wine,' she says,
'is man made divine,' and I may say that if you
have not got the key to these Rabelaisian riddles,
much of the value—the highest value—of the
book is lost to you."

Seeking the meaning of this Bacchic cultus,
this apparent glorification of drunkenness in all
lands and in all times, from Ancient Greece
through Renascent France to Victorian England,
by peoples and persons not themselves given to
excess, he finds it again in the word *ecstasy.*

> We are to conclude that both the ancient people and
> the modern writers recognized ecstasy as the supreme
> gift and state of man, and that they chose the Vine
> and the juice of the Vine, as the most beautiful and
> significant symbol of that Power which withdraws a
> man from the common life and the common conscious-
> ness, and taking him from the dust of earth, sets him
> in high places, in the eternal world of ideas. . .

> Let us never forget that the essence of the book ('Pantagruel') is in its splendid celebration of ecstasy, under the figure of the Vine.

At this point Mr. Machen places the "key" in our hands and declines further to reveal his secrets. In *Mr. Pickwick's* overdose of milk punch we are to find ultimately, "a clue to the labyrinth of mystic theology."

By his own test we are enabled to place Arthur Machen's greatest works on the shelf with "Don Quixote" and "Pantagruel"; by his own test we find the ecstasy of which he speaks in his own pages, under the symbol of the Vine and under figures even more beautiful and terrible.

For minor consideration he finds in Rabelais another symbol of ecstasy:

> The shape of gauloiserie, of gross, exuberant gaiety, expressing itself by outrageous tales, outrageous words, by a very cataract of obscenity, if you please, if only you will notice how the obscenity of Rabelais transcends the obscenity of common life; his grossness is poured out in a sort of mad torrent, in a frenzy, a very passion of the unspeakable."

In Cervantes he finds the greater deftness, the finer artifice, but he believes the conception of Rabelais the higher because it is the more remote. *Pantagruel's* "more than frankness, its ebullition of grossness . . . is either the

merest lunacy, or else it is sublime." And the
thought that succeeds this in the book, sums up
this astonishing philosophy with a conclusion calculated to shock the Puritanic. Thus:

> Don't you perceive that when a certain depth has
> been passed you begin to ascend into the heights? The
> Persian poet expresses the most transcendental secrets
> of the Divine Love by the grossest phrases of the car-
> nal love; so Rabelais soars above the common life,
> above the streets and the gutter, by going far lower
> than the streets and the gutter: he brings before you
> the highest by positing that which is lower than the
> lowest, and if you have the prepared, initiated mind, a
> Rabelaisian 'list' is the best preface to the angelic
> song. All this may strike you as extreme para-
> dox, but it has the disadvantage of being true, and
> perhaps you may assure yourself of its truth by rec-
> ollecting the converse proposition—that it is when
> one is absorbed in the highest emotions that the most
> degrading images intrude themselves.

This fascinating discussion of gods and literature is given the form of a series of rambling
talks by an "obscure literary hermit," whom
Machen pretends to have found in "an almost
mythical region lying between Pentonville and
the Caledonian Road," an excellent setting, as
witness:

> Here, in the most retired street of that retired
> quarter, he occupied two rooms on the ground floor of
> a big, mouldy house, standing apart from the street
> and sheltered by gaunt-grown trees and ancient shrubs;

and just beside the dim and dusty window of the
sitting-room a laburnum had cast a green stain on the
decaying wall. The laburnum had grown wild, like
all the trees and shrubs, and some of its black, strag-
gling boughs brushed the pane, and of dark, windy
nights while we sat together and talked of art and
life we would be startled by the sudden violence with
which those branches beat angrily upon the glass.

In this gloomy sanctuary, lighted by two lonely candles, the "obscure literary hermit" dis-
courses on Casanova and card-sharping, Coleridge and Cervantes, Keats and Shelley, *M. Dupin* and the *Morte d'Arthur,* Rabelais and the
Song of Songs, Catholicism and piano-organs.
Here George Eliot is gibbeted and Charles Reade
glorified, Thackeray earns his spurs as a pamph-
leteer, and *Huck Finn* sails into the harbor of
Farre Joyaunce. There is set forth the enchant-
ment of wine and other high matters, as well as
much admirable criticism of certain lesser literary
worthies, all bearing upon the author's main proposition, the great "distinction."

For the "hermit" and for Arthur Machen,
there are only two solutions of existence, one the
materialistic or rationalistic, the other the spiritual
or mystic, and Man may make his choice. Mach-
en's vote is for the latter: if the former be true
then Keats is lunacy and the *Morte d'Arthur* is
"an elaborate symptom of insanity;" if the lat-

ter, then *Pride and Prejudice* is not fine literature
and the works of George Eliot are "the works of
a superior insect." If rationalism be the truth,
"then all literature, all that both sides agree in
thinking the finest literature, is simple lunacy,
and all the world of the arts must go into the
region of mania."

Again: "Literature is the expression, through
the aesthetic medium of words, of the dogmas of
the Catholic Church, and that which in any way
is out of harmony with these dogmas is not literature;" but "no literal compliance with Christianity is needed, no, nor even an acquaintance
with the doctrines of Christianity. The Greeks,
celebrating the festivals of Dionysius, Cervantes
recounting the fooleries of *Don Quixote,* Dickens
measuring *Mr. Pickwick's* glasses of cold punch,
Rabelais with his thirsty *Pantagruel* were all sufficiently Catholic from our point of view, and the
cultus of Aphrodite is merely a symbol misunderstood and possibly corrupted; and if you can
describe an initiatory dance of savages in the
proper manner, I shall call you a good Catholic."

To the rationalists he presents an examination
paper for their further undoing, thus:

    1.   Explain, in rational terms, *The Quest of the
Holy Graal.* State whether in your opinion such a
vessel ever existed, and if you think it did not, justify

your pleasure in reading the account of the search
for it.

2. Explain, logically, your delight in colour. State,
in terms that Voltaire would have understood, the
meaning of the phrase, "the beauty of line."

3. What do you mean by the word "music"? Give
the rational explanation of Bach's Fugues, showing
them to be as (1) true as Biology and (2) useful as
Applied Mechanics.

4. Estimate the value of Westminster Abbey in
the avoirdupois measure.

5. "The light that never was on land or sea."
What light?

6. "Faery lands forlorn." Draw a map of the
district in question, putting in principals towns and
naming exports.

7. Show that "heaven lies about us in our in-
fancy" must mean "wholesome maternal influences
surround us in our childhood."

Is this nonsense? But what, asks the "hermit,"
is the "rational" explanation of our wonder and
joy at the vision of the hills? "Are a great sym-
phony, the swell and triumph of the organ, the
voices of the choristers, to be tested by the process
of the understanding? . . . But in certain
quarters my problem would be very quickly
solved. I should be told, more in sorrow than in
anger, that my emotion at the sight of certain
shapes of earth was due to the fact that hill air
was highly ozonized, and that the human race had
acquired an instinctive pleasure in breathing it,
greatly to its digestive profit. And if I tried to

turn the tables by declaring that I experienced an
equal, though a different delight in the spectacle
of a desolate, smoking marsh, where a red sun
sinks from a world of shivering reeds, I suppose
I should hear that some remote ancestor of mine
had found in some such place 'pterodactyls plentiful and strong on the wing,' and if I like the
woods it was because a monkey sat at the root
of my family tree, and if I love an ancient garden it is because I am 'second cousin to the
worm.' "

His summary completes the paradox of ecstasy and sin:

> If the science of life, if philosophy, consisted of a
> series of mathematical propositions, capable of ra-
> tional demonstration, then *Pride and Prejudice* would
> be the highest pinnacle of the literary art; but if not,
> if we, being wondrous, journey through a wonderful
> world, if all our joys are from above, from the other
> world where the Shadowy Companion walks, then no
> mere making of the likeness of the external shape will
> be our art, no veracious document will be our truth;
> but to us, initiated, the Symbol will be offered, and
> we shall take the Sign and adore, beneath the outward
> and perhaps unlovely accidents, the very Presence and
> eternal indwelling of God.
>
> We have tracked Ecstasy by many strange paths,
> in divers strange disguises, but I think that now, and
> only now, we have discovered its full and perfect
> definition. For Artifice is of Time, but Art is of
> Eternity.

And so on . . . The sense of the futility
almost of attempting to explain Arthur Machen
becomes more pronounced as I progress. You
will have to read him. You will find his earlier
books (if you are fortunate) in a murky corner,
on the topmost shelf, of some second-hand book-
shop.

OF ARTHUR MACHEN

Arthur Machen was born in Wales, in 1863.
He is married and has two children. He is High
Church, "with no particular respect for the Arch-
bishop of Canterbury," as a friend of his once
remarked, and, of course, he is subconsciously
Catholic, as are all those "lonely, awful souls"
who write ecstasy across the world. He hates
puritanism with a sturdier hatred than inspires
Chesterton; for a brilliant exposition of that
aversion, I commend readers to his mocking introduction to "The House of Souls."

His greatest work was all done before 1900.
This included "The Great God Pan and The Inmost Light" (1894) and "The Three Impostors"
(1895) which later were included, with other
early tales, in "The House of Souls." "Hieroglyphics" and "The Hill of Dreams" also
were done in the eighteen-nineties, although neither found a publisher until some years after the

end of the century. His first book, "The Anat-
omy of Tobacco" (1884), was published anony-
mously; at least, pseudonymically; it bore upon
its title-page the magnificent name of one *Leoli-
nus Siluriensis*. Other labors of his youth were
translations of the *Heptameron,* Casanova, and
Le Moyen de Parvenir of Beroalde de Verville,
all made for daring booksellers who issued them
in limited editions.

"The Chronicle of Clemendy," already mentioned, belonged to this period. It is the Welsh
Heptameron, a chronicle of amorous intrigue,
joyous drunkenness and knightly endeavor that
stands well forward with the world's classics. In
it there is the veritable flavor of mediaeval record.
Less outspoken than the Queen of Navarre and
less verbose than Boccaccio, Machen proves himself the peer of either in gay, irresponsible, diverting, unflagging invention, while his diction is
lovelier than that of any of his forerunners, not
excepting the nameless authors of those rich
Arabian tapestries that were the parent tales of
all mediaeval and modern *facetiae*. That the
Chronicle of Clemendy should have been a publication of the year 1888 is an extraordinary consideration.

Throughout most of this period Machen was a
bookseller's assistant in London, and this associa-

tion and the turn of his reading are reflected in
his work; for all its tragedy, I fancy it was the
happiest time of his life. Occasionally he sold a
short story to some one of the numerous mush-
room journals of the day, and in his leisure moments he wandered about London until his knowledge of that metropolis, like *Mr. Weller's,* was
"extensive and peculiar." In the years of slow
torture that were his creative years, when green
tea without sugar, and dry bread, with tobacco
for dessert, were almost his daily fare, many of
his finest tales and essays were written. They
went for the proverbial song to whichever journal
would take them, and with the proceeds Arthur
Machen bought more tea and tobacco. In a ten
by six garret chamber he labored, dreamer and
mystic; and when the winter nights were cold he
warmed his cramped and stiffened fingers at the
flame of his gas-jet; there was no other fire in
the room. Years of unspeakable terror—and
ecstasy.

When his work was done, which is his own way
of describing the advent of the new century,
Machen turned strolling player and for a time
alternated between the smartest theatres of London and the shabbiest music-halls of London's
East End. Later, he went back to literature (if
he ever had deserted it), and wrote for *The*

Academy and *T. P.'s Weekly*. For some years
he was a descriptive writer on the staff of the
London *Evening News*.

His published work, since his newspaper connection began, includes the famous *Bowmen*,
"The Terror," a brilliant and distinguished mystery novel of the war, "The Great Return," a
remarkable short story in his early manner, "War
and the Christian Faith," and "The Confessions
of a Literary Man." Two of his most beautiful
books, "The Secret Glory" and "Far Off
Things," the latter his autobiography, have just
appeared; the former existed in manuscript for
more than fifteen years. The latter tells the
poignant story of his early years and disappoint-
ments; its sequel, "Things Near and Far," completes one of the saddest stories in literature.

He is still one of the most original and excellent minds of England, and the distinction of
his style and thought is one of the most unmistakable of contemporaneous literary phenomena.

The day is coming when a number of serious
charges will be laid against us who live in this
generation, and some severe questions asked, and
the fact that we shall be dead, most of us, when
the future fires its broadside, has nothing at all
to do with the case.

We are going to be asked, *post-mortem,* why

we allowed Ambrose Bierce to vanish from our
midst, unnoticed and unsought, after ignoring
him shamefully throughout his career; why
Stephen Crane, after a few flamboyant reviews,
was so quickly forgotten at death; why Richard
Middleton was permitted to swallow his poison
at Brussels; why W. C. Morrow and Walter
Blackburn Harte were in our day known only to
the initiated, discriminating few, their fine, gold-
en books merely rare "items" for the collector.
Among other things, posterity is going to demand of us why, when the opportunity was ours,
we did not open our hearts to Arthur Machen
and name him among the very great.

AMBROSE BIERCE

THE MAN

TEN years of speculation and apprehension have passed since the disappearance of Ambrose Bierce. Sanguine hopes long have dwindled, and only the frailest possibility survives that he yet lives in some green recess of the Mexican mountains, or some tropical Arcadia in South America. Assuming that he is dead, as we must assume who do not look for a miracle, he has fulfilled a prophecy made years ago by a writing man of his acquaintance:

"Some day he will go up on Mount Horeb and forget to come down. No man will see his death-struggle, for he'll cover his face with his cloak of motley, and if he sends a wireless it will be this: ' 'Tis a grave subject.' "

There has been no wireless.

There are many persons who do not care for the writings of Ambrose Bierce, and thousands—it is shocking to reflect—who never have heard of him. The Hon. Franklin K. Lane, erstwhile Secretary of the Interior, has gone upon record as thinking him "a hideous monster, so like the mixture of dragon, lizard, bat and snake as to be unnameable," a characterization almost Biercian in its cumulative invective. When Mr. Lane made this remark, or wrote it down (whichever may have been the case), he said it with pious horror and intense dislike; but when Gertrude Atherton asserted that Bierce had the must brutal imagination she had encountered in print, she was paying him a compliment, and she intended to. Out of those two appraisals we may extract the truth—that Bierce was a mighty artist in his field, with little or no concern for the reaction of weaker vessels to his art.

A great many persons knew Ambrose Bierce, and some loved him, and some hated and feared him. All, from their own point of view, had excellent reason for their quality of regard. Save for those who made up this catholic and vari-minded assemblage, few persons can speak of Ambrose Bierce, the man. The story of Ambrose Bierce the novelist, the satirist, the humorist, and the poet, is in a large degree the story of Ambrose Bierce the man; but in a larger degree is the story of Ambrose Bierce the man, the story of Ambrose Bierce the novelist, satirist, humorist, and poet.

It is generally known that he served throughout the Civil War. He emerged a Major, brevetted for distinguished services, and with an honorable scar upon his body. Twice he had rescued

wounded comrades from the battlefield, at the
risk of his life; at Kenesaw Mountain he was
severely wounded in the head. He came out of
the conflict a soldier, with a decided leaning toward literature, and the story goes that he tossed
up a coin to determine his career. Instead of
"head" or "tail" he may have called "sword" or
"pen," but the story does not so inform us. Whatever the deciding influence may have been, Bierce
commenced journalist and author in San Francisco, in 1866, as editor of the *News Letter*. Then,
in 1872, he went to London, where, for four
years, or until 1876, he was on the staff of *Fun,*
edited by the younger Tom Hood.

In London, the editors of *Fun,* amazed at the
young man's fertile ability, conceived the notion
that he could write anything, and accordingly
piled his desk with a weird assortment of old
woodcuts, minus their captions; they requested
that he "write things" to fit them. The "things"
Bierce wrote astonished England, and Pharisees
squirmed beneath his lash as they had not done
since the days of Swift. A cruel finger was on
secret ulcers, and the American's satires quickly
gained for him, among his colleagues, the name
of "Bitter Bierce." The stinging tales and fables he produced to order are those found in the
volume called *Cobwebs from an Empty Skull,*

reputed to be by Dod Grile, and published in
1871. A year previously, he had published *The
Fiend's Delight* and *Nuggets and Dust,* caustic
little volumes largely made up of earlier diab-
olisms from California journals. His intimates
of the period included such joyous spirits as
Hood, George Augustus Sala and Capt. Mayne
Reid, the boys' novelist; this quartette, with
others, frequented a taproom in Ludgate Station, and gave itself over, as Bierce humorously
confesses, "to shedding the blood of the grape."
Thus Bierce:

> We worked too hard, dined too well, frequented too
> many clubs and went to bed too late in the forenoon.
> In short, we diligently, conscientiously and with a
> perverse satisfaction burned the candle of life at both
> ends and in the middle.

He relates some delightful episodes of the
period in his *Bits of Autobiography,* the first volume in his Collected Works; the funniest and
one of the most typical, perhaps, is that concerning his difficulties with John Camden Hotten, a
publisher with whom Mark Twain was having
trouble of his own at about the same time—although at a greater distance. Hotten owed
Bierce money for certain work, and Bierce, usually financially embarrassed, hounded Hotten for
it until the publisher, in despair, sent the im-

placable creditor to negotiate with his (Hotten's) manager.   Bierce talked vividly for two hours, at the end of which time the crestfallen manager capitulated and produced a check already made out and signed.   It bore date of the following Saturday.   The rest of the story belongs to Bierce:

> Before Saturday came, Hotten proceeded to die of a pork pie in order to beat me out of my money. Knowing nothing of this, I strolled out to his house in Highgate, hoping to get an advance, as I was in great need of cash.   On being told of his demise I was inexpressibly shocked, for my cheque was worthless. There was a hope, however, that the bank had not heard.   So I called a cab and drove furiously bankward.   Unfortunately my gondolier steered me past Ludgate Station, in the bar whereof our Fleet Street gang of writers had a private table.   I disembarked for a mug of bitter.   Unfortunately, too, Sala, Hood, and others of the gang were in their accustomed places.   I sat at board and related the sad event. The deceased had not in life enjoyed our favour, and I blush to say we all fell to making questionable epitaphs to him.   I recall one by Sala which ran thus:
>
> > *Hotten,*
> > *Rotten,*
> > *Forgotten.*
>
> At the close of the rites, several hours later, I resumed my movements against the bank.   Too late— the old story of the hare and the tortoise was told again!   The heavy news had overtaken and passed me as I loitered by the wayside.   I attended the funeral, at which I felt more than I cared to express.

The appearance of his *Cobwebs From an Empty Skull* made Bierce for a time the chief wit and humorist of England, and, combined with his satirical work on *Fun,* brought about his engagement by friends of the exiled Empress Eugénie to conduct a journal against her enemies, who purposed to make her refuge in England untenable by newspaper attacks. It appeared that James Mortimer, who was later to found and edit *Figaro,* was in the habit of visiting the exiled Empress at Chislehurst, and he it was that learned of a threat by M. Henri Rochefort to start his paper, *La Lanterne,* in England; Rochefort, who had persistently attacked the Empress in Paris. Mortimer suggested the founding and registering in London of a paper called *The Lantern,* which was done and Bierce was made its editor. But the struggle never came; Rochefort, outwitted, knew the game was up, and did not put his threat into execution, although Bierce, for a few numbers, had the delight of abusing the Frenchman to his heart's content, a pursuit he found extremely congenial.

Bierce the satirist for a time was in his element; but there was little material wealth to be gained in London, and at times he was pretty hard up. He revived his failing fortunes, for a short period, by writing and publishing his series of "Lit-

tle Johnny" stories—humorous, misspelled essays
in zoology, supposed to be the work of a small
boy. These were popular and added color to his
name; but Bierce's mind was now turning backward to the country he had deserted, and in 1876
he returned to San Francisco.

He remained then on the Pacific coast for a
quarter of a century, save for a brief period of
mining near Deadwood, South Dakota, where his
adventures with road-agents and other "bad men"
were hair-raising. On a night in 1880 he was
driving in a light wagon through a wild part
of the Black Hills. The wagon carried thirty
thousand dollars in gold belonging to the mining
company of which he was manager, and beside
him on the wagon seat was Boone May, a famous
gunman who was under indictment for murder.
May had been paroled on Bierce's promise that
he would see him into custody again. The notorious gunman sat, huddled in his rubber poncho,
with his rifle between his knees; he was acting as
guard of the company's gold. Although Bierce
though his companion somewhat *off* guard, he
said nothing.

There came a shout: "Throw up your hands!"

Bierce reached for his revolver; but it was
needless. Almost before the words had left the
highwayman's lips, with the quickness of a cat

May had hurled himself backward over the seat, face upward, and with the muzzle of his weapon within a yard of the bandit's throat, had fired a shot that forever ruined the interrupter's usefulness as a road-agent.

Bierce returned again to San Francisco. Through the warp and woof, then, of certain California journals, for many years, ran the glittering thread of his genius, and to this period belongs much of his finest and strongest work. He became a mighty censor who made and unmade men and women, a Warwick of the pen. It is no exaggeration to say that corrupt politicians, hypocritical philanthropists and clergymen, self-worshipers, notoriety seekers, and pretenders of every description trembled at his name. He wielded an extraordinary power; his pen hung, a Damoclean sword, over the length and breadth of the Pacific coast. Those who had cause to fear his wrath opened their morning papers with something like horror. He wrote "epitaphs" to persons not yet dead, of such a nature—had they been dead—as to make them turn in their graves. Many of his poetic quips were venomous to a degree, and he greeted Oscar Wilde, on the poet's arrival in America, in 1882, with a blast of invective that all but paralyzed that ready wit. His pet abominations were James

Whitcomb Riley and Ella Wheeler Wilcox. In
the earlier days of his power an assault in print
was believed sufficient cause for a pistoled reply,
and Bierce was always a marked man; but he
was utterly fearless, and as he was known to be a
dead shot, himself, his life always was "spared"
by the victims of his attacks. His vocabulary of
invective was the widest and most vitriolic in
modern journalism but it was not billingsgate;
Bierce never penned a line that was not impeccable. His wit was diabolic—Satanic—but he
was always the scholar, and he always bowed po-
litely before he struck. The suave fierceness of
his attack is unique in contemporaneous literature.

He cherished no personal enmities, in the ordinary sense, for his attacks were largely upon
principles promoted by men, rather than upon
the men themselves. One who knew him said:
"I look upon Bierce as a literary giant. I don't
think he really means to walk rough-shod over
people, any more than a lion means to be rough
with a mouse. It is only that the lion wonders
how anything so small can be alive, and he is
amused by its antics." With his clairvoyant vision, his keen sense of justice, and his extraordinary honesty, what an international fool-killer he
would have made!

Yet this fierce and hated lampooner had his softer side, which he displayed to those he loved and who loved him; and these were not too few. One of his oldest friends wrote, in a letter: "His private gentleness, refinement, tenderness, kindness, unselfishness, are my most cherished memories of him. He was deeply—I may say childishly—human. . . It was in these intimate things, the aspects which the world never saw, that he made himself so deeply loved by the few whom he held close. For he was exceedingly reserved. Under no circumstances could he ever be dragged into physical view before the crowds that hated, feared or admired him. He had no vanity; his insolence toward the mob was detached, for he was an aristocrat to the bottom of him. But he would have given his coat to his bitterest enemy who happened to be cold."

His humor, as distinct from his wit, was queer and picturesque, and was a distinguished quality. In his column of "Prattle" in the *San Francisco Examiner,* he once remarked that something was "as funny as a brick ship." A friend giggled with delight at the conception, and repeated it to others; but to his dismay he could find none who would enjoy it. "A brick ship!" they echoed. "That isn't funny, it's simply foolish." Another time, Bierce announced that he regarded every

married man as his natural enemy; and the Phil-
istines raved, saying he was evil, nasty, and a
hopeless beast. The boyish fun of his remarks
seemed always lost on the crowd. Again, when
the missing-word nonsense was going on, he began to say obscure things, in his column, about
a poem which Dr. David Starr Jordan had just
published. At length he inaugurated a missing-
word contest of his own, somewhat as follows:
"Dr. Jordan is a ——, and a ——, and a ——."
He invited the public to send him its guesses.
Heaven knows what replies he received; but the
Professor was worried, and asked Bierce's friends
why the writer was getting after him. Finally
the missing words were supplied: "Dr. Jordan
is a gentleman, and a scholar, and a poet." Bierce
supplied and publish them himself.

Once a lawyer, whose remarkable name was
Otto Tum Suden, broke out with some public
matter that Bierce didn't like. Accordingly, he
wrote a little jingle about Tum Suden, the bur-
then of which was "Tum Suden, tum duden, tum
dey!" It completely silenced poor Tum.

It is not unnatural, however, that Bierce should
have been misunderstood, and people always
were misunderstanding him. Standing, one day,
with a friend, upon a high elevation at a mid-
winter fair, he looked down at a vast crowd

swarming and sweating far below him. Suddenly, coming out of a reverie, he said: "Wouldn't it be fun to turn loose a machine gun into that crowd!" He added a swift and droll picture of the result, which sent his friend into convulsions, the latter knowing perfectly well that Bierce would not have harmed a single hair on a head in that swarm. But suppose his friend had been no friend at all—had just met the writer, and did not know him for what he was! That was Bierce's way, however, and it ran into print. People could never understand him—some people.

Even his friends did not escape his lash. However deep his affection for them, he never spared them in public if they stepped awry. But they were inclined to think it an honor when he got after them in print, and, naturally, there was an admiring literary coterie that hailed him as master. I suspect they flattered him, although I cannot imagine him accepting their flattery. And he *was* a Master. One of this group, perhaps the closest of his literary friends, once sent him a story for criticism. Bierce returned it with the laconic remark that his friend "must have written it for the *Waverly Magazine* when he was a school-girl."

Among his friends and pupils were the poets, George Sterling and Herman Scheffauer, and he was on the best of terms with the Bohemian crowd that made old San Francisco a sort of American Bagdad; but I believe he never participated in their café dinners, where they were gazed at and marveled over by the fringing crowd. He was unconscious of his own greatness, in any offensive sense, and either ignored or failed to see the startled or admiring looks given him when people were told, "That is Ambrose Bierce!" He was not a showman. I have heard it said that women adored him, for he was cavalierly handsome; but he was not much of a ladies' man. As I have suggested, however, he was always a gentleman and gentlemen are none too plentiful.

An especially interesting chapter in his journalistic career began in 1896, when a great fight was being waged in the nation's capital. The late Collis P. Huntington was conducting a powerful lobby to pass his "refunding bill," releasing him and his associates of the Central Pacific Railroad from their obligations to the government. Bierce was asked by William Randolph Hearst to go to Washington for the *Examiner*, to give what aid he might in defeating the scheme.

A Washington newspaper man said to Huntington: "Bierce is in town."

"How much does he want?" cynically asked Huntington.

This insult was reported to Bierce, who replied: "Please to go back and tell him that my price is about seventy-five million dollars. If, when he is ready to pay, I happen to be out of town, he may hand it to my friend, the Treasurer of the United States."

The contest was notable. As in the Eugénie case, Bierce was in his element. He wrote so fast and so furiously that it became a whimsical saying that he wrote with a specially prepared pencil, because his pens became red hot and his ink boiled. The result was happy, whatever he used, for he drove the corruptionist gang out of the Capitol, and forced a withdrawal of the insolent measure. It was not so long ago that the last installment of the entire debt was handed to Bierce's "friend," the Treasurer of the United States.

Later, Bierce removed to Washington, where he spent his last years. He was already a celebrity when he came there to live, and was more or less of a lion; but his anger always was great when he fancied anyone was showing him off. It is said that he indignantly declined to attend a theater with a friend, in New York, because seats had been procured in a box for the party

that was to accompany them. Another story tells
of an alleged scene he made in a Washington
drawing-room, when his host presented a street
railway magnate. The car baron extended his
hand.

"No!" thundered Bierce, in magnificent rage.
"I wouldn't take your black hand for all the
money you could steal in the next ten years! I
ride in one of your cars every night and always
am compelled to stand—there's never a seat for
me."

And the story goes that the black hand was
speedily withdrawn. I do not vouch for the tale;
but it sounds a bit tru-ish, if not entirely so.

It has been remarked time and again that
Bierce was embittered by failure of the world to
appreciate his work; by his "obscurity." That
is untrue. Recognition was slow, but he was
certainly not unknown; indeed if a multiplicity
of attacks upon a man may make him famous,
Bierce was famous. It is the critics who are to
blame for this myth; many attacked him, and
many, eager to help him, spoke mournfully of
his great and unappreciated genius; and after a
time the story stuck. In a breezy jingle, Bierce
himself summed up this aspect of the case, as
follows:

My, how my fame rings out in every zone—
A thousand critics shouting, "He's unknown!"

It is probably true, also, that the foreword to
his first book of stories, *Tales of Soldiers and
Civilians,* had something to do with the legend:

> Denied existence by the chief publishing houses of
> the country, this book owes itself to Mr. E. L. G.
> Steele, merchant, of this city [San Francisco]. In
> attesting Mr. Steele's faith in his judgment and his
> friend, it will serve its author's main and best am-
> bition.

But, as the years went by, the *cognoscenti* came
to know him very well indeed. And those who
knew him best, in his later years, assert that he
was not morose and unhappy, although he was a
considerable sufferer from asthma, and had tried
various climates without result.

His religion, such as it was, was his own, and
had nothing to do with creeds and denominations;
theology he abominated. But Bierce was no
cheap scoffer.

"This is my ultimate and determinate sense of
right," he once wrote. " 'What under the circumstances would Christ have done?'—the Christ
of the New Testament, not the Christ of the
commentators, theologians, priests, and parsons."

And his friend, Edwin Markham, said of him:

"He is a composite mind—a blending of Hafiz

the Persian, Swift, Poe, Thoreau, with sometimes a gleam of the Galilean."

THE MASTER

It seems likely that the enduring fame of the
most remarkable man, in many ways, of his day,
chiefly will be founded upon his stories of war—
the blinding flashes of revelation and interpreta-
tion that make up the group under the laconic
legend, "Soldiers," in his greatest book, *In the
Midst of Life*. In these are War, stripped of
pageantry and glamor, stark in naked realism,
terrible in grewsome fascination, yet of a sinister
beauty. Specifically, it is the American Civil
War that furnishes his characters and his texts,
the great internecine conflict throughout which
he gallantly fought; but it is War of which he
writes, the hideous Thing.

Perhaps it is the attraction of repulsion that,
again and again, leads one to these tales—although
there is a record of a man who, having read
them once, would not repeat the experiment—but
it is that only in part. There is more than mere
terror in them; there is religion and poetry, and
much of the traditional beauty of battle. Their
author was both soldier and poet, and in the war
stories of Ambrose Bierce, the horror and ugli-
ness, the lure and loveliness of war are so blended

that there seems no distinct line of demarcation; the dividing line is not a point or sign, but a penumbra. Over the whole broods an occult significance that transcends experience.

Outstanding, even in so collectively remarkable a group, are three stories, "A Horseman in the Sky," "A Son of the Gods," and "Chickamauga." The first mentioned quietly opens with a young soldier, a Federal sentry, on duty at a point in the mountains overlooking a wooded drop of a thousand feet. He is a Virginian who has conceived it his duty to join the forces of the North, and who thus finds himself in arms against his family. It is imperative that the position of the camp guarded by the young soldier be kept secret; yet he is asleep at his post. Waking, he looks across the gorge, and on the opposite height beholds a magnificent equestrian statue —a Confederate officer on horseback, calmly surveying the camp beneath.

The young soldier, unobserved by his enemy, aims at the officer's breast. But suddenly his soul is in tumult; he is shaken by convulsive shudders. He cannot take life in that way. If only the officer would see him and offer battle! Then he recalls his father's admonition at their parting: at whatever cost he must do his duty. The horseman in gray turns his head. His features are

easily discernible now.   There is a pause.   Then
the young soldier shifts his aim from the officer's
breast and, with stony calm, fires at the horse.   A
moment later, a Federal officer, some distance
down the side of the cliff, sees an amazing thing
—a man on horseback, riding down into the valley through the air.

Here is the conclusion to that story:

> Ten minutes had hardly passed when a Federal ser-
> geant crept cautiously to him on hands and knees.
> Druse neither turned his head nor looked at him, but
> lay without motion or sign of recognition.
>
> "Did you fire?" the sergeant whispered.
>
> "Yes."
>
> "At what?"
>
> "A horse.   It was standing on yonder rock—pretty
> far out.   You see it is no longer there.   It went over
> the cliff."
>
> The man's face was white but he showed no other
> sign of emotion.   Having answered, he turned away
> his face and said no more.   The sergeant did not un-
> derstand.
>
> "See here, Druse," he said, after a moment's silence,
> "it's no use making a mystery.   I order you to report.
> Was there anybody on the horse?"
>
> "Yes."
>
> "Who?"
>
> "My father."
>
> The sergeant rose to his feet and walked away.
> "Good God!" he said.

It may be claimed that the *idea* of this story—
its conclusion—is not original with Bierce.   I

don't know; although for all anyone may say to
the contrary the episode may be a transcript from
life. Certainly, in this form it is original enough.
De Maupassant contrives the same sense of
"shock" in the tale of a sailor who, after years
of wandering, returns to the village of his youth
to find his old home vanished, and who, in consequence, betakes himself to a shadier section
of town. In the midst of his maudlin carousing,
he discovers in the half-naked creature he is fond-
ling, his sister. Remotely, the idea is the same
in both stories, and, I fancy, it antedates De
Maupassant by hundreds of years. *Since* publication of Bierce's tale, young writers in numbers
deliberately have sought the effect (*Peccavi!*)
with tales that are strangely reminiscent; and
Billy Sunday rhetorically tells a "true story" of
the same sort, which might have been taken di-
rectly from the French master. Thus does life
plagiarize from literature, in later days, after literature first has plagiarized from life.

At any rate, it is a situation that was never
better handled, an idea never more cleanly distorted, than by Bierce. "A Horseman in the
Sky" is one of the most effective of his astonishing vignettes, and is given first place in the volume. It has one objection, an objection that
applies to all terror, horror, and mystery tales;

once read, the secret is out, and rereading cannot
recapture the first *story* thrill. It may be, however, that all literature, of whatever classification,
is open to the same objection. Fortunately, as in
the case of Bierce, there is more to literature than
the mere "story."

There is less of this *story* in "A Son of the
Gods," but as a shining glimpse of the tragic
beauty of battle it is, I believe, unique; possibly
it is Bierce's finest achievement in the art of *writing*. He calls it a "study in the historical present
tense." In order to spare the lives of the skirmishers, a young staff officer rides forward toward
the crest of a bare ridge crowned with a stone
wall, to make the enemy disclose himself, if the
enemy is there. The enemy *is* there and, being
discovered, has no further reason for conceal-
ment. The doomed officer, instead of retreating
to his friends, rides parallel to the wall, in a hail
of rifle fire, and thence obliquely to other ridges,
to uncover other concealed batteries and regi-
ments. . . .

The dust drifts away. Incredible!—that enchanted
horse and rider have passed a ravine and are climbing
another slope to unveil another conspiracy of silence,
to thwart the will of another armed host. Another
moment and that crest too is in eruption. The horse
rears and strikes the air with its forefeet. They are
down at last. But look again—the man has detached

himself from the dead animal. He stands erect, motionless, holding his sabre in his right hand straight
above his head. His face is toward us. Now he lowers
his hand to a level with his face and moves it outward,
the blade of the sabre describing a downward curve.
It is a sign to us, to the world, to posterity. It is a
hero's salute to death and history.

Again the spell is broken; our men attempt to
cheer; they are choking with emotion; they utter
hoarse, discordant cries; they clutch their weapons
and press tumultuously forward into the open. The
skirmishers, without orders, against orders, are going
forward at a keen run, like hounds unleashed. Our
cannon speak and the enemy's now open in full chorus;
to right and left as far as we can see, the distant crest,
seming now so near, erects its towers of cloud, and the
great shot pitch roaring down among our moving
masses. Flag after flag of ours emerges from the
wood, line after line sweeps forth, catching the sunlight on its burnished arms. . . .

Bierce has been called a Martian; a man who
loved war. In a way, I think he did; he was a
born fighter, and he fought, as later he wrote,
with a suave fierceness, deadly, direct, unhasten-
ing. He was also an humane and tender spirit.
As typical as the foregoing paragraphs are the
following lines, with which the narrative concludes:

The skirmishers return, gathering up the dead. Ah,
those many, many needless dead! That great soul
whose beautiful body is lying over yonder, so conspicuous against the sere hillside—could it not have been
spared the bitter consciousness of a vain devotion?

Would one exception have marred too much the pitiless
perfection of the divine, eternal plan?

In his more genuinely *horrible* vein, "Chickamauga" is unrivaled; a grotesquely shocking
account of a deaf-mute child who, wandering
from home, encounters in the woods a host of
wounded soldiers hideously crawling from the
battlefield, and thinks they are playing a game.
Rebuffed by the jawless man, upon whose back
he tries to ride, the child ultimately returns to his
home, to find it burned and his mother slain and
horribly mutilated by a shell. There is nothing
occult in this story, but, with others of its *genre,* it
probes the very depths of material horror.

"An Occurrence at Owl Creek Bridge" is better known than many of Bierce's tales, and here
again is a form that has attracted imitators. Like
a pantoum, the conclusion brings the narrative
back to its beginning. A man is engaged in being hanged in this extraordinary tale, and prep-
arations are proceeding in a calm and businesslike
manner. An order is given, and the man is
dropped. . .

Consciousness returns, and he feels the water
about him; the rope has broken and he has fallen
into the stream! He is fired upon, but escapes.
After days of travel and incredible hardship, he

reaches his home. His wife is in the doorway to
greet him, and he springs forward with extended
arms. At that instant, he feels a stunning blow
on the back of his neck, a blaze of light is about
him—then darkness and silence. "Peyton Far-
quhar was dead; his body, with a broken neck,
swung gently from side to side beneath the tim-
bers of the Owl Creek bridge."

Again there is that sense of shock, at the end,
as we realize that between the instant of the
hanged man's drop and the succeeding instant
of his death, he has lived days of emotion and
suspense.

The tales of civilians, which make up the second half of Bierce's greatest book, are of a piece
with his war stories. Probably nothing more
weirdly awful has been conceived than such tales
as "A Watcher by the Dead," "The Man and the
Snake," and "The Boarded Window," unless it
be Stevenson's "The Body Snatcher." The volume entitled *Can Such Things Be?* contains several similar stories, although, as a whole, it is
apocryphal. In "The Mocking Bird" we find
again the *motif* of "A Horseman in the Sky;"
in "The Death of Halpin Frayser" there is a
haunting detail and a grewsome imagery that
suggest Poe, and in "My Favorite Murder," one
of the best tales Bierce ever wrote, there is a

satirical whimsicality and a cynical brutality that make the tale an authentic masterpiece of *something*—perhaps humor!

"A literary quality that is a consecration," remarked one critic, of Bierce's method and method-results. That is better than speaking of his "style," for I think the miracle of Bierce's fascination is as much a lack of what is called *style* as anything else. The clarity and directness of his thought and expression, and the nervous strength and purity of his diction, are the most unmistakable characteristics of his manner.

Bierce the satirist is seen in nearly all of his stories, but in *Fantastic Fables,* and *The Devil's Dictionary* we have satire bereft of romantic association; the keenest satire since Swift, glittering, bitter, venomous, but thoroughly honest. His thrusts are at and through the heart of sham. A beautiful specimen of his temper is the following fable:

An Associate Justice of the Supreme Court was sitting by a river when a traveler approached and said:

"I wish to cross. Would it be lawful to use this boat?"

"It would," was the reply, "it is my boat."

The traveler thanked him, and pushing the boat into the water, embarked and rowed away. But the boat sank and he was drowned.

"Heartless man!" said an Indignant Spectator,

"why did you not tell him that your boat had a hole in it?"

"The matter of the boat's condition," said the great jurist, "was not brought before me."

The same cynical humor is revealed in the introductory paragraphs of a story already referred to, "My Favorite Murder."

The solemn absurdities of the law were Bierce's frequent target; thus, in his *Devil's Dictionary*, the definition of the phrase "court fool" is, laconically, "the plaintiff." His biting wit is nowhere better evidenced than in this mocking lexicon. Bacchus, he conceives to be "a convenient deity invented by the ancients as an excuse for getting drunk;" and a Prelate is "a church officer having a superior degree of holiness and a fat preferment. One of Heaven's aristocracy. A gentleman of God." More humorously, a Garter is "an elastic band intended to keep a woman from coming out of her stockings and desolating the country."

In the same key are his collected epigrams, in which we learn that "woman would be more charming if one could fall into her arms without falling into her hands."

With all forms of literary expression, Bierce experimented successfully; but in verse his percentage of permanent contributions is smaller

than in any other department. His output, while
enormous, was for the most part ephemeral, and
the wisdom of collecting even the least of his
jingles may well be called into question. At least
half of the hundreds of verses contained in the two
volumes of his collected works given over to poetry, might have been left for collectors to discover and resurrect; and some delightful volumes of *juvenilia* and *ana* thus might have been
posthumously achieved for him by the collecting
fraternity. But, "someone will surely search
them out and put them into circulation," said
their author, in defense of their publication in
the definitive edition, and there they are, the
good, the bad, and the indifferent.

Happily, in the ocean of newspaper jingles
and rhymed quips there is much excellent poetry.
Kipling, by some, is asserted to have derived his
"Recessional" from Bierce's "Invocation," a noble and stately poem; and in "The Passing
Show," "Finis Aeternitatis," and some of the
sonnets we have poetry of a high order. Maugre,
we have much excellent satire in many of his
journalistic rhymes. Life Swift and Butler, and
Pope and Byron, Bierce gibbeted a great many
nobodies; but, as he himself remarked, "satire,
like other arts, is its own excuse, and is not de-
pendent for its interest on the personality of

those who supply the occasion for it." If many
of Bierce's *Black Beetles in Amber* seem flat,
many too are as virile and keen as when they were
written; and if he flayed men alive, just as certainly he raised the moral tone of the community
he dominated in a manner the value of which
is perhaps measureless.

The best example of poetry, however, left us
by Bierce, *me judice,* is that great prose poem,
The Monk and the Hangman's Daughter. This
work is the joint production of Bierce and G.
Adolphe Danziger. The latter translated it from
the German of Prof. Richard Voss and, I believe,
elaborated it. Being unsure of his English, Danziger gave it over to Bierce for revision. Bierce,
too, elaborated it, practically rewriting it, he testified, as well as changing it materially. There
was discussion about authorship honors; but the
book is a bit of literary art that is a credit to all
three men, and that would be a credit to six. The
world would be poorer without this delicate and
lovely romance. Saturated with the color and
spirit of the mediæval days it depicts, it is as
authentic a classic as *Aucassin and Nicolette;* and
its *denouement* is as terrible as it is beautiful. The
strange story of Ambrosius the monk, and the
outcast girl Benedicta, "the hangman's daughter," is one of the masterpieces of literature.

Ambrose Bierce was a great writer and a great
man. He was a great master of English; but
it is difficult to place him. He is possibly the
most versatile genius in American letters. He is
the equal of Stevenson in weird, shadowy effect,
and in expression he is Stevenson's superior.
Those who compare his work with that of Steph-
en Crane (in his war stories) have not read him
understandingly. Crane was a fine and original
genius, but he was, and is, the pupil where Bierce
is Master. Bierce's "style" is simpler and less
spasmodic than Crane's, and Bierce brought to
his labor a first-hand knowledge of war, and an
imagination even more terrible than that which
gave us *The Red Badge of Courage.* The hor-
rors of both men sometimes transcend artistic effect; but their works are enduring peace tracts.

It has been said that Bierce's stories are "formula," and in a measure it is true; but the formula
is that of a master chemist, and it is inimitable.
He set the pace for the throng of satirical fabu-
lists who have since written; and his essays, of
which nothing has been said, are powerful, of
immense range, and of impeccable diction. His
influence on the writers of his time, while unac-
knowledged, is wide. Rarely did he attempt anything sustained; his work is composed of keen,
darting fragments. His only novel is a redac-

tion. But who shall complain, when his fragments are so perfect?

THE MYSTERY

In the fall of the year 1913, Ambrose Bierce,
being then some months past his seventy-first
birthday anniversary, started for Mexico. For
some time, and with keen interest, he had followed the fortunes of the revolutionary cause
headed by Francisco Villa; and he believed that
cause a just one. From various points along the
line of his journey, before he reached the southern republic, Bierce wrote to his friends. In
December of 1913, the last letter he is known to
have written was received by his daughter. It
was dated the month of its receipt, and from
Chihuahua, Mexico. In it Bierce mentioned,
casually enough, that he had attached himself,
unofficially, to a division of Villa's army—the
exact capacity of his service is not known—and
spoke of a prospective advance on Ojinaga. The
rest is silence.

No further word, bearing the unmistakable
stamp of authenticity, ever has come out of Mexico. There have been rumors without number,
even long categorical accounts of his death at the
hands of the revolutionists, but all must be called
false. There is in them not the faintest ring of

truth. They represent merely the inevitable speculation, and the inevitable "fakes" of unscrupulous correspondents.   Typical of the innumerable
"clews" offered is the following: One newspaper
correspondent in El Paso reported that a second
correspondent had told him that he (the second
correspondent) had seen and talked with Bierce
before the author passed into Mexico, and that
Bierce had declared he would offer his services
to the revolutionary cause, failing to make which
connection, he would "crawl into some out-of-the-
way hole in the mountains and die."   The author
of these pages hastily communicated with the
second correspondent, and the second correspondent, in a positive communication, vowed that he
never had seen Bierce, nor heard the story of
Bierce's reported utterance.

The most elaborate account of Bierce's
"death" was quoted in full from the *Mexican
Review,* by the *Washington Post,* under date of
April 27, 1919.   Its extraordinary detail gives
it a semblance of truth that other accounts have
lacked, and, without intending to perpetuate a
story that Bierce's friends and relatives do not
for a moment believe, I reproduce it in its un-
grammatical entirety:

> A short time since the *Review* editor was convers-
> ing with a friend, a former officer in the constitutional-

ist army, and casually asked him if he had ever heard
of an American named Ambrose Bierce. To his surprise he replied that he had met him several times
and had become quite well acquainted with him. This
was due to the fact that Bierce could speak little if
any Spanish, while the officer is well educated and
speaks English fluently.

The latter declared that he saw and talked with
Bierce several times in the vicinity of Chihuahua late
in 1913 or early in 1914. Later—1915—he met a
sergeant of Villa's army, an old acquaintance, and
this man told him about having witnessed the execution of an American who corresponded in every manner with Bierce's description.

This affair took place near Icamole, a village in
the region of Monterey and Saltillo, east of Chihuahua state, in August, 1915. The constitutionalists
occupied that village while Gen. Tomas Urbina, one
of Villa's most blood-thirsty fellows, was nearby and
between that place and the border.

One day an American, acompanied by a Mexican,
convoying four mules, on one of which was a machine gun, while the others were loaded with ammu-
nition, was captured on the trail, headed toward Icamole, and taken before Urbina. The Mexican told
Urbina that he had been engaged by another Mexican
to guide the mules and the American to the constitu-
tionalist camp at Icamole. That was all he knew.
The American apparently could not speak or understand any Spanish, and made no intelligent reply to
the questions asked him.

The bloodthirsty Urbina, who was never so happy
as when killing some one himself or ordering it to be
done, wearied of questioning the prisoners and ordered them to be shot at once.

The two were stood up in front of a firing squad,
where the Mexican threw himself on his knees,

stretched out his arms, and refused to have his eyes bandaged, saying he wanted to "see himself killed." All he asked was that his face be not mutilated, which was not done.

Seeing his companion on his knees, the American followed suit, but the Mexican told him to stand up. He did not understand what was said, but remained on his knees, arms outstretched, like his companion, and with unbandaged eyes he met his death at the hands of the firing squad. The two victims were buried by the side of the trail.

The sergeant who witnessed the affair described Bierce exactly, though he had never seen him to his knowledge. Incidentally it may be stated that Urbina himself soon after met his death by Villa's orders at the hands of the notorious "Matador Fierro."

It is to be doubted whether Villa ever knew about this double execution, such affairs being common enough at that time.

Inquiry is now being made for the sergeant in question, in order that further details of the affair may be secured, as well as information regarding the exact locality of the execution and the burial place of the two victims.

Only two things need to be considered in refuting the foregoing narrative. First, this is only one of a great many stories, despite its painstaking vraisemblance; and, second, the execution is dated in the fall of 1915, approximately two years after Bierce's last letter. Had Ambrose Bierce been living in 1915, had he been living at any time between the date of his last letter and the reported date of his death, he would have sent some communication to his friends and relatives. This is recognized by all who knew him best, and is the final answer to the extravagant chronicle in the *Mexican Review*. It may be remarked, however, in passing, that the carefully detailed account is just such a tale as might have been constructed by a press agent eager to lift the onus of Bierce's disappearance from official Mexican shoulders; and of such paid press agents there have been many. It will be noted that care is taken also to report the execution of Urbina, and even to "whitewash" Villa, although I believe the propaganda to have been Carranzista.

This careful piece of imagination was closely followed by a still more carefully elaborated account of the same story. Written by James H. Wilkins, it appeared in the *San Francisco Bulletin* of March 24, 1920. Wilkins quotes George F. Weeks (who was probably responsible for the former story, since he was editor of the *Mexican Review*), speaks of Major Bierce as having been military advisor to Carranza, and dwells at length on Bierce's alleged expressed desire to "die in battle." One Edmundo Melero, an associate editor of the *Mexican Review,* is declared to have been with Bierce almost from the moment of his arrival in Mexico; but as Melero died of pneu-

monia the day after Wilkins arrived in Mexico
City (I am quoting Wilkins' story), Wilkins
could not interview him. Fortunately, Weeks
knew all that Melero could have told, and Weeks
told Wilkins that Melero had been seeking a
Mexican, then in Mexico City, who had been
present at the attack on the mule train when
Bierce was "captured" and "executed."

To find this Indian in a city of a million souls
was no trick for Wilkins, and the discovered eye-
witness repeated the story I have already quoted,
with unimportant variations. The convenient Indian then produced a *photograph* of Ambrose
Bierce, which had been among the effects taken
from the "body." Wilkins identified it at once.
But the Indian would not part with it; he pre-
ferred to destroy the photograph, believing it had
served its purpose, and fearing consequences to
himself when the Wilkins revelation was published. This photograph was the sensation of the
Wilkins story, which otherwise was the same story
as formerly told.

A friend of mine in California fairly rushed
this article to me, saying, "Wilkins is an old and
reliable journalist." I shall attempt to deny neither his age nor his reliability, but I will casually
suggest that *if* he is reliable he is extraordinarily
gullible, whatever his age.

One remarkable story came privately to me,
and was to the positive effect that Ambrose Bierce
had been seen, alive and well, in San Luis Potosi,
as late as December of 1918, five years after his
disappearance and after his last letter to his
friends. The narrator of that tale believed him
still to be living (May, 1920), and ready to come
back and astound the world when his "death"
had been sufficiently advertised. There were
many details to the story, and another Mexican
figured. This Mexican had seen a portrait of
Bierce in the story-teller's office, had exclaimed
at sight of it, and had told of knowing the original; Bierce and this Indian, it developed, had
parted company in San Luis Potosi in December
of 1918! The Major was known to the Mexican
as "Don Ambrosio." But *this* Mexican was murdered in Los Angeles, in a triangular love scrape,
as was attested surely enough by a newspaper
account of his murder, so the narrator's chief
witness had vanished. This investigator, too, was,
at least, too credible, although he was shrewd
enough to see through the Weeks and Wilkins
stories, and to tear them to pieces. Certainly he
knew better than to accuse Bierce of seeking
morbid publicity.

Other extraordinary tales there have been: a
dispatch to the *New York World* of April 3,

1915, dated from Bloomington, Illinois, soberly
recited that Mrs. H. D. Cowden of that city,
Bierce's daughter, had received a letter from her
father which entirely cleared the mystery of his
disappearance. He was even then in France, it
seemed, an officer on Lord Kitchener's staff, had
escaped injury, and was in good health. Yet
from Mrs. Cowden's own lips I have had it that
no such letter, no such information conveyed in
whatever manner, ever reached her. A later
story reported that Bierce had perished with
Kitchener, when the great soldier was drowned.

This is all sensational journalism. There is
every reason to doubt that Bierce ever left Mexico; that he long survived his last bit of letter-
writing—the brief communication to his daughter, in December of 1913. The manner of his
passing probably never will be known, but it is
to be recalled that he suffered from asthma, and
that he was more than seventy-one years of age
when he went away.

There is one further consideration: Did Bierce,
when he went into Mexico, expect to return?
Did he go, calmly and deliberately, to his death?
Did he, indeed, seek death? The question has
been raised, and so it must be answered. In support of the contention, two highly significant
letters have been offered. These were received

by Mrs. Josephine Clifford McCrackin of San
José, California, long a warm friend of the vanished author, and there is not the slightest doubt
of their authenticity. The first, chronologically,
is dated from Washington, September 10, 1913,
and is as follows:

> Dear Joe: The reason that I did not answer your
> letter sooner is—I have been away (in New York) and
> did not have it with me. I suppose I shall not see
> your book for a long time, for I am going away and
> have no notion when I shall return. I expect to go
> to, perhaps across, South America—possibly via Mexi-
> co, if I can get through without being stood up against
> a wall and shot as a gringo. But that is better than
> dying in bed, is it not? If Dunc did not need you so
> badly I'd ask you to get your hat and come along.
> God bless and keep you.

The faint suggestion in this letter is more clearly defined in the second and last letter received
by Mrs. McCrackin, three days later:

> Dear Joe: Thank you for the book. I thank you
> for your friendship—and much besides. This is to
> say good-by at the end of a pleasant correspondence
> in which your woman's prerogative of having the last
> word is denied to you. Before I could receive it I
> shall be gone. But some time, somewhere, I hope to
> hear from you again. Yes, I shall go into Mexico
> with a pretty definite purpose, which, however, is not
> at present disclosable. You must try to forgive my
> obstinacy in not "perishing" where I am. I want to
> be where something worth while is going on, or where

nothing whatever is going on. Most of what is going
on in your own country is exceedingly distasteful to
me.

   Pray for me? Why, yes, dear—that will not harm
either of us. I loathe religions, a Christian gives
me qualms and a Catholic sets my teeth on edge, but
pray for me just the same, for with all those faults
upon your head (it's a nice head, too), I am pretty
fond of you, I guess. May you live as long as you
want to, and then pass smilingly into the darkness—
the good, good darkness. Devotedly your friend.

He goes "with a pretty definite purpose;" his
"obstinacy" will not allow him to perish in Washington, and death at the hands of the Mexicans is
"better than dying in bed." He wishes to be
where something worth while is going on, or
"where nothing whatever is going on;" and, finally, there is the reference to the "good, good darkness."

Yet also he had announced his intention, if pos-
isble, to cross South America.

It is difficult to get away from the hints in
those two letters; and the assumption that Bierce
knew he would not return is inescapable. But to
assume that he cordially sought death is another
matter. He would be ready for it when it came,
he would pass smilingly into the "good, good
darkness;" but does anyone who knows Ambrose
Bierce or his work suppose that he would en-
courage, let us say, his own murder?—that he

would rush into battle, let us say, hoping for a
friendly bullet through his heart?—that his passing was, in effect, a suicide, although the hand
may have been another than his own? Ambrose
Bierce's friends do not think so, and they are
right. His "good-by" to his friends was real
enough, but all he certainly knew was that somewhere, some time, perhaps in a few months, perhaps in a year or two, death would overtake him,
and that he would not have returned to his home.
That death did come to him, not long after he
wrote the last letter received by his daughter, we
must believe.

If he was murdered by bandits, and had a
chance for life, it is safe to assume that there was
a fight. If he died of disease, which is not at all
improbable, he regretted his inability to write.
Bierce was not cruel to his friends.

It is likely that the disappearance is complete,
that the mystery never will be solved. The United States government's investigation has come
to nothing, and indeed it has been lax enough.

Ambrose Bierce was born in Meiggs County,
Ohio, June 24, 1842, son of Marcus Aurelius
and Laura (Sherwood) Bierce. He died—where?
And when? Or is he dead? The time for hope
would seem to have passed. One thinks of that

grim prophecy, years ago; and there has been no wireless.

Setting aside the grief of friends and relatives, there is something terribly beautiful and fitting in the manner of the passing of Ambrose Bierce; a tragically appropriate conclusion to a life of erratic adventure and high endeavor. Soldier-fighter and soldier-writer. Scotson Clark's well-known caricature of Bierce dragging a pen from a scabbard is the undying portrait of the man.

STEPHEN CRANE:
A WONDERFUL BOY

I T hardly profits us to conjecture what Stephen
Crane might have written about the World
War had he lived. Certainly, he would have
been in it, in one capacity or another. No man
had a greater talent for war and personal adventure, nor a finer art in describing it. Few
writers of recent times could so well describe the
poetry of motion as manifested in the surge and
flow of battle, or so well depict the isolated deed
of heroism in its stark simplicity and terror.

To such an undertaking as Henri Barbusse's
Under Fire, that powerful, brutal book, Crane
would have brought an analytical genius almost
clairvoyant. He possessed an uncanny vision; a
descriptive ability photographic in its clarity and
in its care for minutiæ—yet unphotographic in
that the big central thing often was omitted, to be
felt rather than seen in the occult suggestion of
detail. Crane would have seen and depicted the
grisly horror of it all, as did Barbusse, but also
he would have seen the glory and the ecstasy and
the wonder of it, and over that his poetry would
have been spread.

While Stephen Crane was an excellent psy-

chologist, he was also a true poet. Frequently
his prose was finer poetry than his deliberate essays in poesy. His most famous book, *The Red
Badge of Courage,* is essentially a psychological
study, a delicate clinical dissection of the soul
of a recruit, but it is also a *tour de force* of the
imagination. When he wrote the book he had
never seen a battle: he had to place himself in
the situation of another. Years later, when he
came out of the Greco-Turkish *fracas,* he remarked to a friend: *"The Red Badge* is all right."

Written by a youth who had scarcely passed
his majority, this book had been compared with
Tolstoy's *Sebastopol* and Zola's *La Débâcle,* and
with some of the short stories of Ambrose Bierce.
The comparison with Bierce's work is legitimate;
with the other books, I think, less so. Tolstoy
and Zola see none of the traditional beauty of
battle; they apply themselves to a devoted—almost obscene—study of corpses and carnage generally; and they lack the American's instinct for
the rowdy commonplace, the natural, the irrever-
ent, which so materially aids his realism. In *The
Red Badge of Courage* invariably the tone is kept
down where one expects a height: the most heroic
deeds are accomplished with studied awkward-
ness.

Crane was an obscure free-lance when he wrote
this book. The effort, he says, somewhere, "was

born of pain—despair, almost." It was a better piece of work, however, for that very reason, as Crane knew. It is far from flawless. It has been remarked that it bristles with as many grammatical errors as with bayonets; but it is a big canvas, and I am certain that many of Crane's deviations from the rules of polite rhetoric were deliberate experiments, looking to effect—effect which, frequently, he gained.

Stephen Crane 'arrived' with this book. There are, of course, many who never have heard of him, to this day, but there was a time when he was very much talked of. That was in the middle nineties, following publication of *The Red Badge of Courage,* although even before that he had occasioned a brief flurry with his weird collection of poems called *The Black Riders and Other Lines.* He was highly praised, and highly abused and laughed at; but he seemed to be 'made.' We have largely forgotten since. It is a way we have.

Personally, I prefer his short stories to his novels and his poems; those, for instance, contained in *The Open Boat,* in *Wounds in the Rain,* and in *The Monster.* The title-story in that first collection is perhaps his finest piece of work. Yet what is it? A truthful record of an adventure of his own in the filibustering days that preceded

our war with Spain; the faithful narrative of the
voyage of an open boat, manned by a handful of
shipwrecked men. But Captain Bligh's account
of *his* small boat journey, after he had been sent
adrift by the mutineers of the *Bounty,* seems
tame in comparison, although of the two the
English sailor's voyage was the more perilous.

In *The Open Boat* Crane again gains his effects by keeping down the tone where another
writer might have attempted 'fine writing' and
have been lost. In it perhaps is most strikingly
evident the poetic cadences of his prose; its rhythmic, monotonous flow is the flow of the gray
water that laps at the sides of the boat, that rises
and recedes in cruel waves, "like little pointed
rocks." It is a desolate picture, and the tale is
one of our greatest short stories. In the other
tales that go to make up the volume are wild,
exotic glimpses of Latin-America. I doubt
whether the color and spirit of that region have
been better rendered than in Stephen Crane's
curious, distorted, staccato sentences.

War Stories is the laconic sub-title of *Wounds
in the Rain.* It was not war on a grand scale that
Crane saw in the Spanish-American complica-
tion, in which he participated as a war correspondent; no such war as the recent horror. But the
occasions for personal heroism were no fewer

than always, and the opportunities for the exercise of such powers of trained and appreciative understanding and sympathy as Crane possessed, were abundant. For the most part, these tales are episodic, reports of isolated instances—the profanely humorous experiences of correspondents, the magnificent courage of signalmen under fire, the forgotten adventure of a converted yacht —but all are instinct with the red fever of war, and are backgrounded with the choking smoke of battle. Never again did Crane attempt the large canvas of *The Red Badge of Courage*. Before he had seen war, he imagined its immensity and painted it with the fury and fidelity of a Verestschagin; when he was its familiar, he singled out its minor, crimson passages for briefer but no less careful delineation.

In this book, again, his sense of the poetry of motion is vividly evident. We see men going into action, wave on wave, or in scattering charges; we hear the clink of their accoutrements and their breath whistling through their teeth. They are not men going into action at all, but men going about their business, which at the moment happens to be the capture of a trench. They are neither heroes nor cowards. Their faces reflect no particular emotion save, perhaps, a desire to get somewhere. They are a line of men

running for a train, or following a fire engine,
or charging a trench. It is a relentless picture,
ever changing, ever the same. But it contains
poetry, too, in rich, memorable passages.

In *The Monster and Other Stories,* there is a
tale called *The Blue Hotel.* A Swede, its central figure, toward the end manages to get himself murdered. Crane's description of it is just
as casual as that. The story fills a dozen pages of
the book; but the social injustice of the whole
world is hinted in that space; the upside-down-
ness of creation, right prostrate, wrong triumph-
ant,—a mad, crazy world. The incident of the
murdered Swede is just part of the backwash of
it all, but it is an illuminating fragment. The
Swede was slain, not by the gambler whose knife
pierced his thick hide: he was the victim of a
condition for which he was no more to blame than
the man who stabbed him. Stephen Crane thus
speaks through the lips of one of the characters:

> We are all in it! This poor gambler isn't even a
> noun. He is a kind of an adverb. Every sin is the
> result of a collaboration. We, five of us, have col-
> laborated in the murder of this Swede. Usually there
> are from a dozen to forty women really involved in
> every murder, but in this case it seems to be only five
> men—you, I, Johnnie, old Scully, and that fool of an
> unfortunate gambler came merely as a culmination, the
> apex of a human movement, and gets all the punish-
> ment.

And then this typical and arresting piece of irony:

> The corpse of the Swede, alone in the saloon, had its eyes fixed upon a dreadful legend that dwelt atop of the cash-machine: 'This registers the amount of your purchase.'

In *The Monster,* the ignorance, prejudice and cruelty of an entire community are sharply focussed. The realism is painful; one blushes for mankind. But while this story really belongs in the volume called *Whilomville Stories,* it is properly left out of that series. The Whilomville stories are pure comedy, and *The Monster* is a hideous tragedy.

Whilomville is any obscene little village one may happen to think of. To write of it with such sympathy and understanding, Crane must have done some remarkable listening in Boyville. The truth is, of course, he was a boy himself—"a wonderful boy," somebody called him—and was possessed of the boy mind. These tales are chiefly funny because they are so true—boy stories written for adults; a child, I suppose, would find them dull. In none of his tales is his curious understanding of human moods and emotions better shown.

A stupid critic once pointed out that Crane, in

his search for striking effects, had been led into
"frequent neglect of the time-hallowed rights of
certain words," and that in his pursuit of color
he "falls occasionally into almost ludicrous mis-
hap." The smug pedantry of the quoted lines is
sufficient answer to the charges, but in support of
these assertions the critic quoted certain passages
and phrases. He objected to cheeks "scarred"
by tears, to "dauntless" statues, and to "terror-
stricken" wagons. The very touches of poetic
impressionism that largely make for Crane's
greatness, are cited to prove him an ignoramus.
There is the finest of poetic imagery in the suggestions subtly conveyed by Crane's tricky adjectives, the use of which was as deliberate with
him as his choice of a subject. But Crane was
an imagist before our modern imagists were
known.

This unconventional use of adjectives is
marked in the Whilomville tales. In one of them
Crane refers to the "solemn odor of burning turnips." It is the most nearly perfect characterization of burning turnips conceivable; can anyone
improve upon that "solemn odor"?

Stephen Crane's first venture was *Maggie: A
Girl of the Streets.* It was, I believe, the first
hint of naturalism in American letters. It was
not a best-seller; it offers no solution of life;

it is an episodic bit of slum fiction, ending with
the tragic finality of a Greek drama. It is a
skeleton of a novel rather than a novel, but it is
a powerful outline, written about a life Crane
had learned to know as a newspaper reporter in
New York. It is a singularly fine piece of analy-
sis, or a bit of extraordinarily faithful reporting,
as one may prefer; but not a few French and
Russian writers have failed to accomplish in two
volumes what Crane achieved in two hundred
pages. In the same category is *George's Mother,*
a triumph of inconsequential detail piling up
with a cumulative effect quite overwhelming.

Crane published two volumes of poetry—*The
Black Riders* and *War is Kind.* Their appearance in print was jeeringly hailed; yet Crane was
only pioneering in the free verse that is to-day,
if not definitely accepted, at least more than tol-
erated. I like the following love poem as well
as any rhymed and conventionally metrical ballad that I know:

> *Should the wide world roll away,*
> *Leaving black terror,*
> *Limitless night,*
> *Nor God, nor man, nor place to stand*
> *Would be to me essential,*
> *If thou and thy white arms were there,*
> *And the fall to doom a long way.*

"If war be kind," wrote a clever reviewer, when the second volume appeared, "then Crane's verse may be poetry, Beardsley's black and white creations may be art, and this may be called a book";—a smart summing up that is cherished by cataloguers to this day, in describing the volume for collectors.   Beardsley needs no defenders, and it is fairly certain that the clever reviewer had not read the book, for certainly Crane had no illusions about the kindness of war.   The title-poem of the volume is an amazingly beautiful satire which answers all criticism.   It should be apropos, just now:

Do not weep, maiden, for war is kind.
Because your lover threw wild hands toward the sky
And the affrighted steed ran on alone,
Do not weep.
War is kind.

> *Hoarse, booming drums of the regiment,*
> *Little souls who thirst for fight,*
> *These men were born to drill and die.*
> *The unexplained glory flies above them,*
> *Great is the battle-god, great, and his kingdom—*
> *A field where a thousand corpses lie.*

Do not weep, babe, for war is kind.
Because your father tumbled in the yellow trenches,
Raged at his breast, gulped and died,
Do not weep.
War is kind.

Swift blazing flag of the regiment,
Eagle with crest of red and gold,
These men were born to drill and die.
Paint for them the virtue of slaughter,
Make plain to them the excellence of killing
And a field where a thousand corpses lie.

Mother whose heart hung humble as a button
On the bright splendid shroud of your son,
Do not weep.
War is kind.

Poor Stephen Crane! Like most geniuses, he had his weaknesses and his failings; like many, if not most geniuses, he was ill. He died of tuberculosis, tragically young. But what a comrade he must have been, with his extraordinary vision, his keen sardonic comment, his fearlessness and his failings!

Just a glimpse of Crane's last days is afforded by a letter written from England by Robert Barr, his friend—Robert Barr, who collaborated with Crane in *The O'Ruddy,* a rollicking tale of old Ireland, or, rather, who completed it at Crane's death, to satisfy his friend's earnest request. The letter is dated from Hillhead, Woldingham, Surrey, June 8, 1900, and runs as follows:

My Dear——

I was delighted to hear from you, and was much interested to see the article on Stephen Crane you sent me. It seems to me the harsh judgment of an unappreciative, commonplace person on a man of genius. Stephen had many qualities which lent themselves to misapprehension, but at the core he was the finest of men, generous to a fault, with something of the old-time recklessness which used to gather in the ancient literary taverns of London. I always fancied that Edgar Allan Poe revisited the earth as Stephen Crane, trying again, succeeding again, failing again, and dying ten years sooner than he did on the other occasion of his stay on earth.

When your letter came I had just returned from Dover, where I stayed four days to see Crane off for the Black Forest. There was a thin thread of hope that he might recover, but to me he looked like a man already dead. When he spoke, or, rather, whispered, there was all the accustomed humour in his sayings. I said to him that I would go over to the Schwarzwald in a few weeks, when he was getting better, and that we would take some convalescent rambles together. As his wife was listening he said faintly: 'I'll look forward to that,' but he smiled at me, and winked slowly, as much as to say: 'You damned humbug, you know I'll take no more rambles in this world.' Then, as if the train of thought suggested what was looked on before as the crisis of his illness, he murmured: 'Robert, when you come to the hedge—that we must all go over—it isn't bad. You feel sleepy—and—you don't care. Just a little dreamy curiosity—which world you're really in—that's all.'

To-morrow, Saturday, the 9th, I go again to Dover to meet his body. He will rest for a little while in England, a country that was always good to him, then to America, and his journey will be ended.

I've got the unfinished manuscript of his last novel here beside me, a rollicking Irish tale, different from anything he ever wrote before. Stephen thought I was

the only person who could finish it, and he was too ill
for me to refuse.   I don't know what to do about the
matter, for I never could work up another man's ideas.
Even your vivid imagination could hardly conjecture
anything more ghastly than the dying man, lying by
an open window overlooking the English channel, re-
lating in a sepulchral whisper the comic situations of
his humorous hero so that I might take up the thread
of his story.

From the window beside which I write this I can see
down in the valley Ravensbrook House, where Crane
used to live and where Harold Frederic, he and I spent
many a merry night together.   When the Romans occupied Britain, some of their legions, parched with
thirst, were wandering about these dry hills with the
choice of finding water or perishing.   They watched
the ravens, and so came to the stream which rises under
my place and flows past Stephen's former home; hence
the name, Ravensbrook.

It seems a strange coincidence that the greatest
modern writer on war should set himself down where
the greatest ancient warrior, Cæsar, probably stopped
to quench his thirst.

Stephen died at three in the morning, the same
sinister hour which carried away our friend Frederic
nineteen months before.   At midnight, in Crane's four-
teenth-century house in Sussex, we tried to lure back
the ghost of Frederic into that house of ghosts, and
to our company, thinking that if reappearing were
ever possible so strenuous a man as Harold would
somehow shoulder his way past the guards, but he
made no sign.   I wonder if the less insistent Stephen
will suggest some ingenious method by which the two
can pass the barrier.   I can imagine Harold cursing
on the other side, and welcoming the more subtle assistance of his finely fibred friend.

I feel like the last of the Three Musketeers, the

other two gone down in their duel with Death. I am
wondering if, within the next two years, I also shall
get the challenge. If so, I shall go to the competing
ground the more cheerfully that two such good fellows
await the outcome on the other side.

Ever your friend,
ROBERT BARR.

The last of the *Three Musketeers* is gone, now,
although he outlived his friends by some years.
Robert Barr died in 1912. Perhaps they are still
debating a joint return.

There could be, perhaps, no better close for a
paper on Stephen Crane than the subjoined paragraph from a letter written by him to a Rochester editor:

"The one thing that deeply pleases me is the
fact that men of sense invariably believe me to
be sincere. I know that my work does not amount
to a string of dried beans—I always calmly admit
it—but I also know that I do the best that is in
me without regard to praise or blame. When I
was the mark for every humorist in the country,
I went ahead; and now when I am the mark for
only fifty per cent. of the humorists of the country, I go ahead; for I understand that a man is
born into the world with his own pair of eyes, and
he is not at all responsible for his vision—he is
merely responsible for his quality of personal
honesty. To keep close to this personal honesty
is my supreme ambition."

THE PASSING OF
JAMES BRANCH CABELL

I COME at once to bury Caesar and to praise him.

With a delightful and ironic gesture of farewell, Cabell has announced his own passing. . . "for oblivion has its merits, to which I now direct a brightening eye." Rather violently, he pushes through the swinging doors so that, with the appearance of accident, they rush back and take his latest and most distinguished detractors across the bridge of the nose. "Vale!" his voice sounds mockingly from the other side; and outside in the fierce light of contemporary journalism stand those who waved him determined farewell, looking, it must be admitted, a bit bewildered and foolish.

I had not read this delicious trifle* when I contemplated my own *Hic jacet,* and a tardy perusal reveals that I have been anticipated in a number of observations; undismayed, I shall go forward with those fragments of my programme that are left me.

It is perfectly obvious, of course, that Cabell

Exit, reprinted in *The Lineage of Lichfield.*

does not for a moment believe in his own report
of Cabell's passing. But the fact is, in an important sense Cabell *is* dead. Sorrowfully I say
it; yet paradoxically am I reconciled and even
happy. Whether his death may be attributed to
natural causes or to the "assassinatory labors"
of his critics need not concern us at this time.
He is dead. In spite of the satirical gayety of
his *ante-mortem* statement, I choose to accept
the report as authentic for reasons which I shall
set forth at length and with what perspicacity is
given me. If the case is not precisely as I state
it, certainly it ought to be, for art and tradition
demand it.

Like Arthur Machen, his one contemporary
in the curious field in which his finest work has
been done, Cabell had a task to perform; like
Machen, he has performed it, and now retires.
The rest may not be silence; but the great books
are written. Already, Cabell "belongs to the
ages."

Cabell's march toward the heights began with
his first published short story, indeed with his
first unpublished manuscript; it ended triumph-
antly upon his objective pinnacle with the ill-
fated "Jurgen." "Figures of Earth" is admirable but, in the light of "Jurgen," apochryphal, as
will be regarded all future writings from Dum-

barton Grange; it marks the first downward step
on the other side of the mountain. Because it is
the first, it is still well toward the summit, and
will remain one of the first half dozen of Cabell's
works. Properly, it immediately should have
preceded "Jurgen," the book with which the master "peaked," to use the language of mortality
statistics. I think there will not be too many to
follow; Cabell is too much the complete artist to
permit dilution of his reputation. To continue,
he must in large measure re-write himself, and
this, I fancy, he is unwilling to do.

The great books are "The Cream of the Jest,"
"Beyond Life," and "Jurgen." Not too far below stand "Figures of Earth," "The Cords of
Vanity," and "Domnei," a magnificent second
line of defense. And the lesser writings are only
lesser because they are not the equal of those
named.

The question I set myself to answer before setting down these impertinent and oracular *dicta,*
was (I suppose *is*) : would Cabell have gone farther had not "Jurgen" been suppressed? I decided that he would not. What further might he
have done? In "Jurgen" he has given the world
a book to stand with the literary bibles of the
ages. At what conceivable peak might he have
aimed his sandals after "Jurgen"? That was the

situation as I saw it, a situation perhaps born of my own violent affection for "Jurgen." There is a limit (I said) even to the genius of a Cabell. Somewhere genius much reach the end of its journey, granting that itself may not recognize that point when attained, and that its performance never can equal the splendor and perfection of its dream—the truth of the latter proposition being responsible for the former. "Jurgen," then, in my opinion, stands with the supreme works of literature; to surpass its performance Cabell would have to achieve something greater than the greatest; and such is my thought of "Pantagruel" and "Pickwick," and "Don Quixote" and "The Queen Pedauque," and a scant handful of others, that I refused to believe the phenomenon possible. This, of course, is reckless and dogmatic; but no matter.

Cabell, therefore, is dead, and while I am sorry yet am I glad, for the great works are written; we shall always have them; nothing can take them from us or from those who are to come after us. I am glad that they were written in my day, and by an American—not, heaven knows, for patriotic reasons; but because the miracle has happened in a country where literature of the sort is sadly needed, and where, perhaps of all nations, it seemed less likely that it immediately could happen. Cabell will write other books, and they will be good books "for one so dead;" he will re-write his earlier books, and may conceivably spoil some of them; but he will never injure his greater fame, for he is too fine an artist. It may be that some day he will approximate "Jurgen" (for in what other direction can he turn? He can not write of Winesburg, Ohio), and give us a posthumous child of the glorious and disreputable pawnbroker; and certainly I believe we shall have further fine tales of the "Gallantry" and "Domnei" persuasion; but at his height he will no more than re-write "Jurgen" with a new carbon in his typewriter.

And so I await the resurrection, hoping that I am wrong.

No other writer of modern times has been in turn so neglected, so bepraised and so bespattered. For twenty years, not all of them apprentice years, he was ignored; suddenly he was discovered and exalted; last week he was villified and condemned. Now, being dead, his apotheosis begins, or, at any rate, is resumed at the point where the kindly office was interrupted by the "bubble-prickers." He has been called many things. Mr. R. M. Lovett, not unkindly, would have him a "decadent realist;" but he is not decadent, and certainly he is not a realist in the

ordinary meaning of that abused word. Mr.
Hewlett, most unkindly, would have him a pre-
tentious charlatan, and a charlatan is the one
thing he is not, even if we grant all the rest. Mr.
Le Gallienne would have him insincere, and finds
that "Jurgen," "The Cords of Vanity" and "The
Soul of Melicent" (*Domnei*), "are as little ani-
mated by any least particle of himself as—any
of his writings;" yet Mr. Lovett discovers that
"throughout all he has remained himself." Mr.
Le Gallienne, again, finds him lewd; but Mr.
Rascoe vigorously asserts the contrary. Into at
least one of Cabell's tales, Mr. Markham reads
a pious moral; but to Mr. Mencken Cabell is a
genial pessimist, an exhilarating skeptic, and
quite the last fellow to point a moral. It is this
last-named notion, surely, that is responsible in
large measure for Mr. Mencken's enthusiastic acceptance of Cabell—one of the most astonishing
episodes in contemporaneous criticism. But it is
perfectly clear from the foregoing, and a great
deal more that might be cited to the same effect,
that any person may read into Cabell whatever
he chooses to read, may look for anything he
would like to find and be reasonably certain of
finding it. This in itself is significant.

Two appreciators have come close to the truth:
Mr. Hugh Walpole and Mr. Wilson Follett.

Mr. Follett's opinion has been frequently quoted, but may be quoted again: "He (Cabell) is a realist of the realities which have nothing to say to fashion and change, and his momentary function among us is to reconstitute that higher realism which is the only true romance." And Mr. Walpole discovers that Cabell is "engaged in the history of the human soul. . . His books are simply varying chapters of the Wandering Jew . . . behind the ephemeral body the features of the longing, searching, questing soul are the same."

Cabell has discovered, or re-discovered, the admirable doctrine (the Economic theory of literature, he calls it) that fine literature must, in effect, be an allegory and not the careful history of particular persons. Thus, often, we glimpse his mysteries through a glass, darkly; his characters in romance have the semblance of shadows within a dream, beckoning and curiously beguiling and always vaguely familiar; his truths flash suddenly upon us, often in retrospect, like the tardy recollection of a half-remembered face in a crowd; and their sum is the sum of reality, sketched with dainty malice in mediaeval colors. The procession of life pours past as we stand at the curb, a grotesque masquerade, a sixteenth century pageant, pennons flying and trumpets singing, quarreling men and weeping women, whispering lovers and boisterous blades, politic friars and haggard kings; but the faces of the company are our own, smirking, wailing, loving, longing. . .

But the denounced gospel of James Branch Cabell most clearly is set forth in his own testaments. "Beyond Life" is studded with revealing texts. . . "Man alone of animals plays the ape to his dreams;" "it is by the grace of romance that man has been exalted above the other animals;" "in youth all men that live have been converts, if but in transitory allegiance, to that religion of the world's youth, to the creed of *domnei,* or woman-worship;" "Art must deal with contemporary life by means of symbols;" and, finally . . . "To what does the whole business tend?—why, how in heaven's name should I know? We can but be content to note that all goes forward, toward something. . . It may be that we are nocturnal creatures perturbed by rumors of a dawn which comes inevitably, as prologues to a day wherein we and our children have no part whatever. It may be that when our arboreal propositus descended from his palm-tree and began to walk upright about the earth, his progeny were forthwith committed to a journey in which to-day is only a way-station.

Yet I prefer to take it that we are components of an unfinished world, and that we are but as seething atoms which ferment toward its making, if merely because man as he now exists can hardly be the finished product of any Creator whom one could very heartily revere. We are being made into something quite unpredictable, I imagine: and through the purging and the smelting, we are sustained by an instinctive knowledge that we are being made into something better. For this we know, quite incommunicably, and yet as surely as we know that we will to have it thus. And it is this will that stirs in us to have the creatures of earth and the affairs of earth, not as they are, but 'as they ought to be,' which we call romance. But when we note how visibly it sways all life we perceive that we are talking about God."

In "The Cream of the Jest," we find this: "It is only by preserving faith in human dreams that we may, after all, perhaps some day make them come true." And there is Horvendile's declaration at Storisende (*ibid*) that we dreamers hunger for we know not what, and for the exercise of powers we know that we possess, without knowing what they are. These are all clews to the Cabell *mystery,* and there are some hundreds of others in the thirteen volumes through which

Cabell's eternal figure, not too carefully disguised, pursues his way adown the centuries. Oh, there are plenty of clews; and you and I, who are the readers, with Cabell the writer, and his central figure, who is all of us put together, must run them down or ever the mystery be solved. Do you remember the mad detective chase in Chesterton's gigantic conception, "The Man Who Was Thursday"? In a sense, Cabell's tales are all detective stories of that sort, and if the quarry be not God, under whatever name, I have misread the allegory, for so, indeed, in a passage I already have quoted, it is explicitly stated . . . The eternal Quest!

Or will you say that "Beauty" is the word? Cabell, of course, will not quarrel with you if you do. He offers you a clew in those curious hieroglyphics which are the frontispiece to "The Cream of the Jest," and which, turned upside down, present the following clarifying legend:

> James Branch Cabell made this book so that he who will may read the story of man's eternally unsatisfied hunger in search of beauty. Ettarre stays inaccessible always and her loveliness is his to look on only in his dreams. All men she must evade at the last and many are the ways of her elusion.

But "beauty" is a comprehensive word . . . and the solution is still far to seek, even after we have glimpsed it. *Jurgen* looked upon strange scenes; his opportunities were many—but he returned at length to his home and his wife, still wondering, still doubtful, and vaguely satisfied with things as they were. Kennaston, in "The Cream of the Jest," also played at detective; and, near the end, the author says: "The Wardens of Earth sometimes unbar strange windows, I suspect—windows which face on other worlds than ours; and They permit this-or-that man to peer out fleetingly, perhaps, just for the joke's sake; since always They humorously contrive matters so this man shall never be able to convince his fellows of what he has seen, or of the fact that he was granted any peep at all." The parable, it it apparent, is constructed on the Hans Christian Andersen formula; if you insist upon a moral, you must sense it; it is not set down in explicit black and white; and when you have discovered it, perhaps it is not the right moral; but still . . .

This is the essence of Cabell's skepticism.

Romantic ironist? Perverse allegorist? Skeptic, mountebank, dreamer? What would you! Is it not enough to understand without understanding? Certainly Cabell is a supreme ironist, and he is also a tender poet. Disillusioned, yes: Cabell is disillusioned; but he is the victim of a greater illusion than any he has lost. Will you call him an anachronism, or the prophet of a new renaissance? Perhaps that does not matter either; probably he is neither the one nor the other, but one of those lonely, occasional figures who, in one guise or another, by sorcery or by satire, offer the world a new meaning of Ecstasy, a new clew to Mystery, and then pass on. Of these, each has his converts and disciples, and . . . "we must be content to note that all goes forward, toward something . . ."

But it must be clear that this denounced gospel of Cabell's is not as perverse and monstrous a thing as those who have failed to read him would have you believe. There is, of course, *Jurgen,* that disreputable pawnbroker; he was suppressed in covers; but you are *Jurgen,* and you would fiercely resent, and very properly so, the suppression of yourself. You are immoral, and therefore *Jurgen* is immoral; but if you are not, *Jurgen* is not. . . Cabell discovers his symbols in curious places, and his interpretations may startle, but they are part of revelation. If naturalism is art in "L'Assomoir" and in "Maggie," it is trebly so in its glorified and interpreted manifestations in "Jurgen." There is, of course, no answer to the determined and illiterate attitude that cries "depravity" in the teeth of *Jurgen's* robustious and healthy adventure; no answer other, at least, than that of Baudelaire to the shocked bleatings of those who were dismayed by accounts (largely false) of Poe's personal "depravity"—"What then?" asked the Frenchman, with a shrug. In such fashion, I reply to those who recount, not without gusto, the several infamies of *Jurgen*.

The chiefest difficulty of the critic would seem to be in distinguishing between the utterances of the author and the utterances of one of the author's puppets. But the "hero" of the piece may be no less the author himself than the "villain," granting that both are Cabell, or whom you will. Mr. Le Gallienne errs here; to show that Cabell is something of a cad, he quotes the episode of Elena Barry-Smith in "The Cords of Vanity," at the conclusion of which the composite hero-villain, Townsend, having languidly insulted the lady of his immediate *affaire,* is ordered from the premises. . .

' "Get out of my house!" Elena said, quite splendid in her fury, "or I will have you horse-whipped. I was fond of you. You would not let me be in peace. And I didn't know you until to-night for the sneering, stuck-up dirty beast you are at heart—" She came nearer, and her glittering eyes narrowed. "And you have no hold on me, no letters to blackmail me with, and

nobody anywhere would take your word for anything against mine. You would only be whipped
by some real man, and probably shot. So do you
remember to keep a watch upon that lying, sneering mouth of yours! And do you get out of
my house!" '

But Cabell wrote the lines I have just quoted
quite as much as what had gone before. Is he any
less Elena Barry-Smith than Robert Townsend?
Is he not, as a matter of fact, simply the omnis-
cient and thoroughly capable author whose genius has given him understanding of the minds
and souls of all his book people, the "good" and
the "bad" alike? Indeed, is it not the very proof
of this genius that the caddishness of the temperamental Townsend is able to infuriate Mr. Le
Gallienne? No, "The Cords of Vanity" is an
important chapter in Cabell's "history of the human soul," which is not to say that Townsend is
not frequently a cad, for he is philanderer, liber-
tine and cad, and, by the same token, not an unfamiliar figure in life. As a study of what is
popularly called "the artistic temperament," the
book is infinitely more revealing than "Dorian
Gray," because it is far less an imaginary biography than Wilde's opus. In "The Cords of Vanity," too, I find a fine flavor of the picaresque
romances of earlier days; there is, artistically, a

joyous rascality, a large unscrupulousness, about
Townsend that is almost epic; for all his weaknesses, or because of them, he is a most likeable
scoundrel.   One may enjoy reading about him
without wishing him for an intimate. The several Cervantesque qualities I find in this book
also are found in "The Rivet in Grandfather's
Neck," with other signs of the Spaniard's thought
and manner.

   If in the two books I have just mentioned, and
in "The Eagle's Shadow," Cabell's three "modern novels," the author seems somewhat less at
ease than in his "mediaeval stories," to divide the
bibliography into its superficial groups, it is because he is largely unconcerned with matters of
immediate and topical interest, save as they re-
late to those "realities which have nothing to say
to fashion and change."   Indeed, Cabell's economic theory, as set forth in "Beyond Life," in
part asserts that first-class art does not reproduce
its contemporary background, and the dictum—
while I, for one, do not subscribe to it without
reservation—may be accepted as the author's own
criticism of his "modern novels." Cabell prefers
the glamor of old days, the colored perspective,
and an atmosphere unbreathed of human lungs,
to paraphrase a line of his own; the mythologies
of all lands and times fascinate and delight him,

and when they are insufficient to his purpose he
invents his own mythology. All to considerable
purpose. In every writing he seems at once seek-
er and interpreter; himself groping toward glam-
or . . . perfection . . . himself revealing his discoveries as they are made. Scorner and
satirist of theology, yet not quite the complete
skeptic; a whimsical pessimist, a fantastic doubt-
er, and completely the victim of a dream that no
disillusion can overcome. . . A watcher of
the skies. Although not quite his greatest book,
"The Cream of the Jest" is the perfect revelation
of James Branch Cabell; of yourself and myself, and of all of us who do not contract from
our associates our opinions and beliefs as if they
were the measles.

I have said that one reads what one will
into Cabell, and it may be that I am doing just
that; but if so, I find what I seek because it is
there.

A detailed review of his books is beside the
point; that is not the purpose of this paper,
which, it is to be remembered, is in the nature of
a memorial. "Our sole concern with the long-
dead is aesthetic," he himself has written, and if
Cabell's death is of recent occurrence, no matter;
I shall anticipate posterity; aesthetic consideration of his books requires only an emotional un-

derstanding of their sum. . . ' "Off-hand,"
began John Charteris, "I would say that books
are best insured against oblivion through practice
of the auctorial virtues of distinction and clarity,
of beauty and symmetry, of tenderness and truth
and urbanity . . ." If this be true (*vide
Beyond Life*), are not the books of James Branch
Cabell insured against oblivion?

Mr. Mencken's famous fulminations against
the south, I believe, were uncalled for and unde-
served, although his praise of Cabell is fulsome
and deserved. Would he have "the Sahara of the
Bozart" as prolific a breeding-ground of medioc-
rity as the north? "The south begins to mutter,"
he says, with jovial, oracular patronage, although
his own ominous murmur for some years has been
heard across the land. . . But if the desert
bloom only once in a century and bring forth a
Poe or a Cabell—or, indeed, a Mencken—it
should be cause for rejoicing. Let us be thankful
for the jungle and sand and the hot, bare middle
years, while with eagerness we await the next
phenomenon. Poe and Cabell are almost the
two most distinguished figures in American literature. Is it significant that both are—were—
southerners? And is not no literature preferable
to the oceans of toilet water literature manufac-
tured in the north?

In the case of Cabell, claquery has been cried
by the "bubble-prickers;" but that is patently
absurd when it is recalled that for twenty years
he was unappreciated and obscure. After a score
of years, a comparatively few intelligent readers
and critics forced Cabell's contemporaneous fame,
over the tumultuous log-rolling of hacks and fools
for lesser men. Now the reaction, dating from
the "Jurgen" episode, and the air is filled with
tiny gloatings. Little critics, obscenely writhing,
wrathfully contemplate the astounding phenomenon of genius . . . amoebas fearfully concerned with the mechanism of an airplane. . .

The situation is not without precedent in history. The eclipse is partial and temporary. "Our
moral prejudices fail to traverse the corridors of
time."

"MICHAEL WOOD" AND THE "INCOMMUNICABLE"

"If in this world there is one misery having no relief, it is the pressure on the heart from the Incommunicable. And if another Sphinx should arise to propose another enigma to man—saying, what burden is that which only is insupportable by human fortitude? I should answer at once: It is the burden of the Incommunicable."—THOMAS DeQUINCEY.

SOME years ago, at a clearance sale of books, chiefly, I believe, of books that would not sell, I purchased for the American equivalent of a "song of sixpence," a duodecimo volume entitled *The Willow Weaver and Seven Other Tales,* by Michael Wood. Something about the appearance of the volume, the style of the writer (as suggested by a hasty perusal of occasional paragraphs), and the curious allure of the story-titles, drew me to it. I had never heard of Michael Wood, and did not then know, as now, that the name should be written in quotation marks. I read the book.

Then, after a lapse of months, I read nine other books by that author in rapid succession. The lapse was occasioned by the fact that no one else, apparently, had heard of Michael Wood, and that I was a long time in bringing together

105

the other volumes signed with that name. When they came, they came together, and from London.

If, by this, I have managed to suggest that the first collection of tales pleased me, and that the rest of Michael Wood's work, when it arrived, continued to please me, I confess that has been my intention. Indeed, I was fascinated.

It is a pity that one may not stop at that; that, having testified to one's extreme liking for a writer, one must explain why, and point out the excellences, and find public explanations for the symbols, in that writer's pages. If it were possible to say, merely, "These are works of extraordinary merit," and then retire, with the assurance that one had said enough to excite public curiosity, the business of literary criticism would be much simplified. Unfortunately, one's lone word is insufficient; it is challenged by the casual reader, and by the critic's own colleagues of the craft. One must give reasons, and, in the case of Michael Wood, that is just what it is difficult to do, for while the surface reasons are sufficiently obvious, there are deeper reasons which have to do with what De Quincey called the "Incommunicable."

Michael Wood is a woman. She is one of the few women I have read who is an artist with words, and not, by the same token, hard, brilliant, and possessed of an opal for a heart. Behind the artist there is the woman, and behind the woman there is—well, it is only fair to say at the outset that Michael Wood is a *religieuse,* and allow opportunity for those canny readers to run, who object to the word God. For Michael Wood is a mystic of mystics, a High Church mystic, I think, although once I thought her a theosophist, and, more than once, a Roman Catholic. Indeed, she is something of all three; and there is an occult beauty about some of her passages, which, ordinarily and easily, we speak of as pagan. It is dangerous too closely to connect an author and his work, and one hesitates to suggest that the extraordinary experiences recited in Michael Wood's stories have been her own; but for the fact that they are founded on experience we have her own assurance. Almost without exception, they are studies of the conflicting powers of good and evil, visible and invisible, as they affect the lives of her various characters; and they offer a solution to certain obstinate questionings which, try as we may, refuse to be stilled.

The sense of the invisible, the intimate understanding of what Arthur Machen calls, simply, "the other things," are here for those who have what the French describe as the "seeing ear and the hearing eye," and to those who understand the appeal is diverse but unmistakable; in the delicate descriptions of nature's most intimate charms, in the color of sound and the sound of color, and in the secret light of a far radiance —evidences of a mysticism that the most pronounced materialist cannot ignore. The characters through whose moods her revelations are vouchsafed, through whose "strangenesses" the arresting quality of her work is made possible, are specimens at whom doctors might elevate their brows (save perhaps Irish doctors, not too far gone with science); they are children with the gift of clairvoyance, possessed of "the sight"; men described as having "the look of eternal childhood on their faces, and the fairy fire in their eyes"; men and women conscious of a measureless Power working in and through them, "fused and remade in a crucible of the Spirit, a cup of the Holy Graal." Such folk, indeed, as often we call "halfwits," or, more charitably, "innocents," whose eyes have the appearance of looking upon things invisible to us, and who hold converse, after darkness has fallen, with the "little people" of hill and plain.

Those are only some of Michael Wood's characters, however. Too, there are many quite "human" persons in her pages. Neither the man, *March,* nor the boy, *Perry,* in a tale called "The

Bending of the Twig" (one of the "seven other
tales"), was able to see the curious things the
child, *Dennis,* saw; both were entirely normal
and "human." Yet the man March flogged the
child for lying, while the boy Perry, sympathiz-
ing, dimly understanding, groped for solution,
and ultimately was the cause of the man's shame-
faced half-surrender. The attitudes of March
and Perry are typical of the intolerance, and the
finer tolerance, of many thousands of persons,
whose lives are touched by manifestations beyond
their ability to credit, and while the moral is obviously that furnished Horatio by the Prince of
Denmark, it is an excellent one, and the story is
admirably done. Other eminently "human" per-
sonages enter the tales, although for the most
part they serve as foils for more remarkable characters whose prescience goes beyond ordinary
experience. *David Alison,* a lovable individual,
a naturalist and author, who occurs in several of
the novels, lingers happily in memory as hovering
intellectually somewhere between the known and
the unknown lands. Certainly, *Alison* had flung
open strange shutters and looked upon secret
things, but he was far from "mad"—unless it be
madness to loathe commercialism and the city,
and to love nature and the fields. And *Father
Anthony Standish* of the *House of Peace,* a very

remarkable character indeed, and Michael Wood's chief creation, is one of the most human and humane figures in recent fiction. Father Standish, in his simple wisdom, knew a great deal better than to believe anybody mad, whatever he might say or do.

This Father Standish is an extraordinary person. He occurs in more than half of Michael Wood's tales; and it is, in part, this trick of the author, constantly to reintroduce her familiars in successive stories, that makes for her unusual plausibility in difficult circumstances. Father Standish, Alison, and half a dozen others, weave through her various books like a hidden cipher, connecting the volumes by a thread of association, the cumulative effect of which, after six or seven appearances, carries a conviction of reality that banishes fiction from the mind. Father Standish, as Warden of the House of Peace, a sort of Quietist retreat, and an asylum for persons weary of the agony of living, is the main influence for good in the narratives he enters; and his rule of intercessory and contemplative prayer is shown by the author to operate as a real and active force of singular potency. To his friendly sanctuary come dreamers of strange dreams, and broken, tired men, fleeing from themselves and from the world. In *The Penitent of*

Brent, it is *Jesse Cameron* who seeks refuge, while beyond the walls he is called "murderer"; in *The House of Peace* (which should be read first), comes *Gereth Fenton,* seeking *Truth;* in *The Mystery of Gabriel,* it is *Gabriel Forraner,* possessed of a strange devil, and seeking he knows not what until he finds it; and in *The White Island* (the latest volume, chronologically), it is *Réné Clinton,* whom, for a certainty, physicians would call a halfwit, but whom Father Standish calls "an instrument of God." Come, too, sometimes, the Playwright and the Doctor, to discuss metaphysics with the wise priest, and others from the outer world, on various missions, but all in search of something incapable of discovery by familiar paths, and incapable of solution by standards known to the material world. Through these lives and these stories moves Father Anthony Standish, the ideal friend, the ideal priest, with no hint about him of the evangelist and little of the preacher; at home in the drawing-room and upon his knees, seeing no visions himself, but accepting without cavil, and with entire belief and sympathy, the strange reports of others.

There is nothing particularly eerie about any of these tales, occult as is their background; rather, one reads in a sort of wonder, like a child occupied with a fairy tale. Neither (and this is important) is there much sermonizing. In a sense, every page is a sermon in little, and many of the conventional words appear, which, used by a less skilful artist, might make of the production an intolerable piece of "goody-good"; but Michael Wood is concerned with incredible secrets, only half revealed . . . suggested by the green fire of Spring, the bubbling note of a thrush, the rush of rain, the color and contour of a cloud, and all the mystery of star-set space and pulsing earth; suggested also by the strange effect of these phenomena upon certain of Nature's favored children, more sensitive than most to the evidences of the ancient enigma and its solution. In contrast to these high lights, there are quaint, subtle, often ironical, etchings in shadow of the humbler life of communities, and of the activities of little *Milors* and *Miladies*. It is all quite admirably done, with few false touches, and few words to spare.

Recently, a young critic, reviewing *The White Island,* thought the author's powers of invention not very pronounced, and the book, as a novel, almost to a lack a *raison d'être.* He could not find much "story," and so, for him, the book failed. He was an unhappy choice to review a book as suffused with mysticism as is this one.

Réné Clinton, pursued by his ineffable vision of a "white island," is, for our critic, less of an "invention" than, perhaps, Rider Haggard's "She." It is, of course, needless to point out that the movement of the *story* is not the most important part of *The White Island*. One feels sorry for a reader who demands a carefully involved and ingenious plot, in which the characters melodramatically vanish and reappear, and the chapters end on exclamation points, and who fancies that sort of thing the highest form of novel-writing.

In spite of the quiet excellence of her novels, however, I am inclined to like best the short stories of Michael Wood, as found in *The Willow Weaver, The Saint and the Outlaw,* and *The King Predestinate*. Here, her precise and delicate characterization is seen to best advantage— in little. "The Mystery of the Son of Man," in the first of the volumes mentioned, is one of the finest short tales I have read in any language, a piece of mediaeval "remembering" with the flavor and authenticity of a Franciscan legend. Other extraordinary stories are "The Excellent Versatility of the Minor Poet," perhaps the most ironic of them all; "Lox," a powerful and moving dog story; "The Prince and the Water Gates," "The Teller of Drolls," and "The Tumultuous Shadows." Those titles alone should be sufficient to send a discerning reader after the books. The last four mentioned occur in *The Saint and the Outlaw.*

Occasionally, it should be said, Michael Wood offends artistically by her use of a hackneyed situation. Thus, in her novel, *The Double Road,* there is a young man falsely accused of theft, but accepting the stigma to shield the actual thief, a girl. Stated baldly, that way, it sounds pretty sentimental and conventional, and, I confess, I like it least of her stories. Still, the author's fine sense of beauty, and her love of nature and humanity, pervade it . . . and prospective readers may be glad to know that the young man does *not* marry the girl.

Michael Wood's style is a very simple and beautiful thing, and, casting about for its inspiration, one finds it, without surprise, in the Bible. Many fine artists have gone to the Bible, and where the experiment has been successful, usually it has been noteworthy. But Michael Wood is a quite conscious artist, selecting and arranging her words and phrases with meticulous care. I shall quote three passages; the first from an allegorical tale, with a natural biblical fervor to it. Thus:

> Now the other traveller passed into profound musing, till his outer senses were locked as though in sleep; and he saw the place in which he was after the

following manner and semblance. He saw the girdle of trees as the wall of a great temple, wherein there were three courts, and at the center a shrine. In the first court was the image of a woman bearing a child in her arms; about her were lights burning and the smell of incense, and the song of human praise; priests in rich vestments celebrated solemn rites, and worshippers, both male and female, old and young, bowed down before this mother and child. In the second court there was a dimness as of a starlit night; there was no incense save the smell of earth and flowers, no song but the song of birds, and of streams, and the boom of waves like the tones of an organ; no lights but strange fires that gleamed and flickered through the night, no worshippers save dim forms of the gracious "hidden peoples," the gods of wood and orchard, plain and tilth. . .

And here is a description of a storm:

At last he slept; and he woke to a wild rush of rain. The wood was full of pale cool light; the pine-needles dripped; he heard the gurgle of a hurry of water in the ditch beyond the gate. He got up; the livid greenish-purple clouds were rushing across the sky; the island was veiled in a white mist of rain; the forest ponies galloped for some scant shelter; some of the herd turned disconsolate noses from the rush of waters; some squealed and kicked and bit at each other; others endured in meekness. A big ants' nest near the gate was flooded; pools stood in the heather; and a heap of cream-white foam swirled on the brown water in the ditch. Light wisps of cloud fled across the background of livid green-purple. He stood under shelter of the trees and watched the storm. . .

It passed; the clouds flew seawards; the sky grew pale even grey; then a cool, soft wind began to blow.

The east grew faint pink, then yellow-grey; then a long line of light quivered over the heather. The new day had come. The birds were stirring and singing; the rabbits hopped out to feed; a stoat darted across the track; and the clang of a cow-bell echoed across the moor.

Again:

All that he saw of the world of day, or of the world of night, was fair, so that the man's soul was steeped in beauty. Sometimes he saw silent, dew-drenched, star-lit English meadows; sometimes grey headlands, with a black foamless sea crawling and heaving below; sometimes strange winding water-ways, stretches of sand, blanched in the moonlight, and eerie with strange wailing songs and elfish voices; sometimes great ruined cities lying in strong sunlight, and barren mountain sides with great caverns therein and twisting spiral stairways winding upwards, whereunto he could not tell; but never a human voice, nor human eyes looking into his; he never saw the gatherer of herbs, save only that he was waiting below his window always when he set forth on his wanderings, and half sprang, half floated out into the moon-shimmer; when he had once set forth he was alone with the speechful, speechless things he loved. . . One day he stood in the silent circle of the dead oaks and watched the dry branches gleam against the sky. He had been there since dawn, lying motionless on the turf, watching all the changes of the day. The sun set, the shadows swooned into the dark, the owls began to hoot among the dusky trees. . .

All this, I submit, of its kind is admirable; and I have deliberately selected at random. Throughout all the tales of Michael Wood there

are these significant descriptions of nature, and
they are strangely moving. For the most part,
the shorter they are the more are they arresting;
and none are particularly long. Often, in a single line, she summons a remote radiance of that
"light that never was on land or sea," and her
people are never far from one or the other, from
forest or ocean, hill, valley or stream.

"Diamonds from a rustic mine," her stories
have been called; but they are gems too little
sought.

In this sophisticated day, it is almost literary
heresy to find praise for a writer on religious subjects. "Art for art's sake," an excellent doctrine
when understood, has become the cheapest of
cant, a catchphrase of the opportunist followers
of fantastic "movements." But in Michael
Wood, even the most violent "Art for art's-sak-
er" may find much to admire, while followers of
an older fashion will find some refuge from a
ruined physical world, and not a little mental
retirement.

One feels indeed, that Father Standish's House
of Peace would be a pleasant institution to have
located not too far from one's own dwelling.

THE ART OF W. C. MORROW

"LOOKING at my friend as he lay upon my bed, with the jewelled knife-handle protruding from his breast, I believed that he was dying. Would the physician never come?"

Chancing, in book or magazine, upon a story whose opening lines were those quoted above, how many readers would turn the page without reading on? How many would close the volume or journal containing it? Not one in a million, I venture to think. In its way, this introductory paragraph is perfect. A complete correspondence course in short-story writing often would tell a student less than a thoughtful consideration of those two sentences. Few more dramatic story-openings have been written.

There is more than a flavor of Poe in the lines; they are almost perfectly in the Poe spirit; Poe in the half whimsical, half sinister mood of "The Cask of Amontillado." But Poe did not write them; they are the first two sentences in a story contributed years ago to a California journal by William Chambers Morrow.

They might also have been written by Ambrose Bierce, whose method—a singularly effective one—was to seize the bare facts of a tragedy

at the moment of its supreme emotion, and from
that point present them stripped of explanatory
influences. Having named Poe and Bierce, one
must turn to France and Guy de Maupassant for
the third and only other man in modern letters
whose urge may have gone into the making of
W. C. Morrow.

Of those three masters of the *conte cruel,* the
influence of Bierce is most apparent throughout
the volume of Mr. Morrow's tales. One naturally looks for it, fortified by the knowledge that
Morrow was the friend and pupil of the older
man; and it is there.

William Chambers Morrow lives* in San Francisco, where his best work was done in the brilliant 'nineties, when that city was the Bagdad
of America and the Mecca of *les jeunes* of
America's writing world. The story with whose
opening lines this appreciation begins was called
"A Peculiar Case in Surgery," after the antique
and curious fashion of describing a tale in its
title. Later, with thirteen others equally good
—some indeed better—it was printed in a volume
published by the Lippincotts, intriguingly called
"The Ape, the Idiot, and Other People." In the
volume thus brought forth, the story was en-

*Mr. Morrow died on April 3, 1923, at Ojai, California.

titled "The Permanent Stiletto," and some
changes were made in the quoted lines as well as
in the body of the narrative; a change decidedly
for the better in the case of the title, and somewhat for the worse in the matter of the introductory paragraph. But it would be difficult, in
whatever manner, to spoil the story, which is a
strange and terrible study of a man who lived his
life with the blade of a stiletto imbedded near his
heart. That, at least, is the story as nearly as I
can tell it without entirely spoiling it for readers
who, after reading this, may care to look up the
original. The conclusion is as startling as the
beginning.

The first story in the book is "The Resurrection of Little Wang Tai," and Mr. Holbrook
Blinn will do well to read it when again he seeks
material for his one-act thrillers. In it an escaped
circus ape and an idiot lad, run away from an
asylum, join forces in as mad and grotesque a
series of adventures as a teeming fancy could
conceive, ending their extraordinary pilgrimage
at a Chinese burying ground where a baby girl
is being interred. The element of horror in the
tale is excellently subdued by the author's humor
and reticence. . . In "The Monster-Maker,"
in which there is less of both humor and reticence,
the effect of the author's stark simplicity of style

coupled with his astonishing plausibility is appalling. "The Monster-Maker" is not Mr. Morrow's finest, but in many ways it is his most arresting tale. Stevenson, who wrote "The Body-Snatcher," perhaps the most appalling thing in literature, might have contrived the Morrow story more artistically had it occurred to him; but he never conceived a greater or more fantastic horror.

Again, in "The Faithful Amulet," Mr. Morrow's admirable reticence is displayed in the handling of a shocking conception—rather, a series of shocking episodes, culminating in an astounding climax—which might have been merely revolting but is actually highly dramatic and moving. Too, there is a queer, ironic humor in the tale that is, despite its blood-dripping, almost diverting. In no other story, I think, is the author's frantic fancy so progressively evident.

In each of these fourteen tales there is an element of horror, rather perhaps of terror, but not all are horror stories. Terrible and beautiful are his stories called "The Hero of the Plague" and "The Inmate of the Dungeon"; and many will name these his finest efforts. Few more poignant characters have been revealed than "The Hero of the Plague," the released convict, subdued and

submissive, at whose heels drag an imaginary ball
and chain, which he must pick up, now and again,
to hasten his steps. Once read, it is a story never
to be forgotten. With its companion story, "The
Inmate of the Dungeon," it is a protest more
powerful than a century of sermons.

"Over an Absinthe Bottle," while the situation
is not entirely new, is still a noteworthy flight, in
which I fancy I find the influence of both Bierce
and De Maupassant. To readers familiar with
the former's story entitled "An Occurrence at
Owl Creek Bridge," the *dènouement* will be less
surprising than to others. . . Two men, mor-
bidly desperate, gamble fiercely over a bottle of
absinthe, drinking steadily the while; and huge
sums of money change hands, although one of
them is penniless and starving. Having won all
his companion's money, the penniless one then
loses it on a throw. The other falling into a
hideous doze, however, the vagrant steals the treasure and starts out to conduct high carnival in the
city with his suddenly-acquired wealth. In the
end detectives find them sitting as they began,
facing each other across a table, and each stone
dead. Neither had stirred from his seat. The
exploit of the penniless one, nefariously wealthy,
all had occurred in the fleeting instant of an abnormal dream—a moment before death froze him

in his chair. . . It is always an effective imposture, and seldom has it been more effectively used.

This is the sort of thing that prating magazine editors call "hoaxing the public"—a sin which one of them defined for me, once, as "the cardinal offense in literature." The cardinal offense in literature is a magazine editor with that kind of a mind.

Mr. Haniel Long, an extremely able critic to whom I recommended Mr. Morrow's stories, found them supreme in imagination and lacking in "passion." Unless I misunderstand his use of the word "passion," he was deceived by the simplicity of Morrow's style which I have already remarked. Morrow attempts no rhetorical flights and he abjures the hysterical exclamation point. It is this relentless simplicity in the handling of abnormal situations by which, it seems to me, he gains his chiefest effect. The cumulative effect of short sentences and unaffected Anglo-Saxon always is likely to be overwhelming, if only the writer be an artist.

The fame of W. C. Morrow, when it arrives, in all probability will be builded upon the fourteen short tales in the "Ape-Idiot book," as its author cheerfully calls it. Gathered from the files of obscure California journals and placed

between covers in 1897, these stories occasioned
some interest in America and a number of flat-
tering reviews; but there was no permanent stir,
and on the whole the venture was not a publisher's
success. In England and France the author was
hailed with complete enthusiasm, and for a time
he wrote for the European market; his tales
were translated into French and appeared in the
leading French journals. But to the American
reading public, Europe—like the war in its early
stages—was "three thousand miles away." The
audience at whose hands he should have received
his kindest treatment accorded him his worst.
His financial returns were slight and he faced
the necessity of earning a living by others means.
He wrote other books—a long short story called
"A Man: His Mark," which should have been
only a short short-story; "Lentala of the South
Seas," a thriller for boys, and "Bohemian Paris
of Today," a good chronicle based, I believe, on
a French work; also several textbooks, including
one on a new system of punctuation—but as the
years passed he wrote less and less, and at length
(I risk my friend's displeasure), slipped into that
graveyard of genius, the correspondence school
of fiction. He was successful; he has turned out
brilliant pupils; but that is hardly a matter of
profound satisfaction to those of us who prefer

the master to the pupils, excellent indeed as are
some of the writings of James Hopper and Cald-
well Dobie. The situation, however, should not
be irremediable—and I believe Morrow has a
trunkful of manuscripts.

Almost as I write, comes news that France, at
least, has not forgotten. A few months ago William Chambers Morrow was elected a member of
the *Societe Academique d'Histoire Internation-
ale*. There are sonorous intellectual organizations
in America, but I have not heard that he has been
invited to join their membership.

ARTHUR COSSLETT SMITH

HIGH time it is someone wrote something about Arthur Cosslett Smith. There are quite too few living writers of the first rank for one to be ignored, and Cosslett Smith, who was born in 1852, can't go on living forever—in the flesh, at any rate. Perhaps a little enthusiasm on our part may win for us another book of tales before the pen is laid aside. That were a reward worth working for.

Few writers with the ability to write well have produced so little work. Two volumes only bear testimony to Mr. Smith's genius; two volumes, containing eight brief tales, and a few short stories in *Scribner's Magazine* which have not yet appeared between covers. "The Monk and the Dancer" was published in 1900; "The Turquoise Cup" three years later. Occasionally one encounters these volumes in the second-hand shops; less often in someone's library, and their failure often to turn up must be significant. The original editions surely numbered not less than 1,000 copies each, and one of the books, at least, has gone into a second edition. The inference is that purchasers are pleased with their buy and are holding the books. But why, if that is true,

is not this writer better known? Why is there
no Twistian cry for more?

The reason may be his slender output and a
conviction that he is dead. Two volumes in seventeen years, and none at all since 1903, is a pretty slim record. The discriminating reader has a
valid objection to register; Mr. Smith has not
treated him fairly. Ordinarily, I would place
the entire blame for the neglect of a writer upon
the public; the great herd of mentally unwashed
who prefer the type of story that films well. In
the case of Cosslett Smith, much of the blame,
at least, attaches to himself. He has been too
good an economist. I like a good economist, God
knows! He who will not write save when he
has a story to tell, or something very definite
to say, merits our highest respect. We love Lamb
with an intenser devotion for that his production
was so meager, quantitatively. But Mr. Smith
has overdone the matter of reticence.

I wrote him once; it was after reading his two
books, and in the course of a search for more.
In his reply he set forth that his story writing
was a sort of recreation in the intervals of more
important labors. Then I learned that he was
a lawyer. Good Lord! More important! The
country is choked with bleating lawyers and
every succeeding year produces its new crop as

regularly as the lilacs bloom and the radishes push through the sod. But there is no surplusage of writers of the Cosslett Smith variety; these do not jostle in the courtrooms or collide in the street. Where did he get this unthinkable notion about his profession?

As for the people, it may be that in reading him they found such delight in the stories that they forgot to notice how excellently well they were done. There are other writers who camouflage their genius in this fashion; Conan Doyle, for instance, in his earlier field.

Cosslett Smith's outlook on life is delightfully un-American, as un-American as James Branch Cabell's, although Cabell, of course, is mediæval, and Smith is at least as modern as the eighteen-nineties. When I say un-American I mean, of course, nothing invidious; merely that his style is not nasal and that it is obviously his theory that literature need not uplift anybody to be very good literature indeed. His characters have not "brave, honest ears," of the adult Horatio Alger, Jr., variety, and they talk perhaps more as people should talk than as people do talk. Indeed, I fancy he resembles Stevenson more closely than another—the Stevenson of the "New Arabian Nights." From all of which you will gather, doubtless, that he is inclined to be a bit

artificial, and as there is nothing quite so artificial
after all, as life, we shall not quarrel if you do.
In his artifice, at any rate, he is a very considerable artist.

Essentially, he is a writer of *contes* in the
veritable French manner, and there is a delicate
Gallic wit and malice in his lines in such tales as
"Trot, Trot to Market" and "The Senior Reader," the scene of neither of which, however, is
France, but, in both cases, England. The hard,
satirical brilliance of some of his dialogue is as
clever as anything in "Dorian Gray" or "The
Green Carnation." And in these tales, by his
cynical sprightliness, he achieves a style that
glitters like electric clusters on champagne. In
another vein, but with the same certain touch, in
the story called "Some Old Families," he satir-
izes a phase of American life in devastating fashion.

But Cosslett Smith is not always the mocking
satirist; it is in a tale of love that he reaches his
finest height—"The Monk and the Dancer," a
masterpiece of short fiction if any has been written in this country; the story of the monk, *An-
gelo,* and what came of his love for *Dolores,* the
dancer. This, it seems to me, is one of the finest
short tales we have had in years; as lovely a thing
spiritually and stylistically as "The Monk and

the Hangman's Daughter," by Bierce and Danziger; a classic of the "Aucassin and Nicolette" type, but with a dash of Boccaccio. . .Tempted by the handsome creature come to the Algerian monastery on a travelers' day, the young monk steals away from the cloisters by night and follows her into the world only to find that he is but another of her toys. After the torture and the agony he returns. . .

> They could hear him splashing through the pools of water that lay upon the rain-drenched road. The moon shone out from between the edges of the clouds, and the Abbot saw the figure of a man approaching. It came on slowly. . . . The footsteps came close up to the gate, then stopped; a pale, drawn face was thrust between the bars and a faint voice whispered, 'Open.' . . . Angelo breathed sobbingly, as if he had been running.
>
> 'Quick!' he gasped, throwing himself against the gate, 'shut it and keep it out!'
>
> 'What!' asked Brother Ambrose.
>
> 'The world,' said Angelo; 'it is pursuing me.'
>
> They shut the gate and locked it.

This is a magnificent tale, magnificently told. The cool silence of the cloisters and the hot flame of tropical suns is in the splendid sweep of it. In sonorous passages the author carries on; his description of the abbey garden under an Algerian moon and other bits of word painting are as gorgeous as a canvas by Maxfield Parrish; his sensing of the souls under the brown cassocks is shrewd and tender; only a great artist could have accomplished the perfected chiaroscuro of this novelette. . . To be sure there is always something fascinating in the amours of a monk. In youth we read French court memoirs secretly and with delight, and are convinced that the Abbés have all the best of it; but this transcends fleshly ecstasies. There is a spiritual glamour and beauty about the tale that allures as seductively as do its worldly phases. To me it appears a genuinely great piece of literature.

Another remarkable story called "The Desert" reveals to the reader something of the monk's ancestry. The stories are quite independent of each other and indeed they are best not read chronologically; still the trick of introducing the characters of one tale into another is intriguing to a degree. Cabell does it with haunting effect and suggests an inter-relation between his tales that baffles and charms like the evidences of a secret cipher. Cosslett Smith does it less often and less effectively, perhaps, but he has only two books to Cabell's eight or nine.

"The Turquoise Cup" is a triumph of light writing, as deft, witty, and bubbling a confection as one will care to read; while in "The Eye of the Harem" I wonder if I have not found the original tale from which some half a dozen sentimental imitations have been made for the movies? "The Peach," the only other tale unmentioned as yet, is a fantastic horror story, told with a lightness of touch that makes it the more effective in connection with its contrasting subject-matter.

Here is a genuine artist who is being much neglected, partly, perhaps, because of his own indifference. It is beside the point, however, that he rates himself too modestly. If there were to be a sufficiently vociferous appeal it is conceivable that he might catch an echo of the uproar in his Rochester home and give us another collection of stories. If, in spite of such an appeal, he continued to refuse, he should be incarcerated in some pleasant *cuartel* and made to write.

Meanwhile old magazines are hard to find and the least his publishers can do is give us between covers those still uncollected tales from the files.

TWO SUICIDES

THE great number of unhappy young artists—poets, painters, composers, *et sic de similibus*—who have perished by their own hand and desire, tempts one to a belief in the suggested affinity between genius and suicide. One might work a passable epigram out of the thought that often genius must prove its existence, paradoxically, by destroying itself. Fortunately, the greater number of artists, young and old, happy and unhappy, whom the world has agreed to call geniuses, who have died tranquilly in bed of disease or old age, forbids a full acceptance of the ingenious theory. In spite of which, the list of self-slain artists is sufficiently moving to arouse interest in motives and causes.

The keyword, of course, is *genius*. A young poet destroys himself; at once we begin to speak of him as a genius. Before this shocking *dènouement,* usually, we have spoken little of him in any connection. Was suicide, then, the proof of genius, or the sensational hollo required to call attention to genius?

Having defined genius as exalted intellectual power, capable of operating independently of tuition and training, and marked by an extraordi-

nary faculty for original creation, we think of
a person tagged with the epithet as one in advance of his fellows and his day, and consequent-
ly somewhat of an eccentric—a position strength-
ened, it must be admitted, by the recorded peculiarities of our oldest established "geniuses."
From this thought it is only a step to believing
genius slightly akin to insanity, and another step
to believing the terms synonymous.

The belief in the last notion but one, is still
widespread among persons who will be the first
to deny the converse of the proposition—that in-
asmuch as a genius is something of a lunatic, a
lunatic is necessarily something of a genius. If
the one always is true, I see no reason for denying the other; but I do not for a moment believe
the one always to be true. Suicide, however, to
the many is the final proof of insanity, and, therefore, in a writing man (or a painting man) of
genius.

The mistake seems to arise from thinking of
genius, perforce, as manifesting itself by what
we are pleased to believe eccentric signs. Seeking with obscene eye for strangenesses in the advertised genius, we find them easily enough, and
when he has closed his life by taking it, we understandingly nod, as much in triumph as in
pity. Now, at length, we know him for the ge-

nius that he is; he has attested his right to the
name. Crime, insanity, voluntary isolation, these
are significant signs; *felo de se* is proof. *Voila!*
a new genius is added to our interesting gallery,
and our pleasant faith in our own anserine judgment again is confirmed. Meanwhile, the excellent fellow who has not yet been driven to this
final act, wants our encouragement, and continues to want it. To obviate an easy rejoinder,
it freely may be granted that eccentricity may be
purely a pose; but, even so, it may cloak genius.
And eccentricity may also cloak—merely eccentricity. The incredible folly is that of making
hard and fast rules for anybody.

Now the truth must be that some geniuses (I
have begun with this word, and so I shall continue to use it, although I do not particularly
like it) are insane and some are not—a commonplace; but are we to insist that only he shall be
called insane who has found unbearable "the
intolerable evil called life"? It may be indeed
that genius of a certain order is closely akin to
insanity, and when a youth sings lovingly of
Death the paramour, then woos and wins the sable embrace, one is fortified in the belief; yet such
terms as "morbid" and "unhealthy" are more or
less arbitrary, and the youth himself will tell you
that they have nothing to do with art. Beauty

for him is a comprehensive word, and he finds beauty where he will.

For many persons who are too greatly obsessed by Gautier's doctrine of "art for art's sake," the suicide of a young artist is the perfect conclusion, the consummate touch necessary to round out a brief and tragic existence, leaving its fame a thing of slight and sinister beauty—as complete and perfect in little as a sonnet or a cameo. Similarly, the assassination of Lincoln, for them, while deplorable on a number of counts, is the perfect solution: it ends his history with artistic completeness, and leaves his life a faultless poem. Thus we see in operation an aesthetic Destiny, terribly at work on human lives, and deeply concerned lest a false nuance shall mar the pitiless perfection of its art.

All this is fascinating and dangerous and highly immoral. One may speak of morality in this connection, perhaps, without inviting a sneer. To be specific, at this point, one does not contend that suicide is either moral or immoral; but the thought which would make of suicide a splendid and ineffable thing is as vicious and immoral as it is perilously alluring.

Hubert Crackanthorpe went to his death in the River Seine at the age of 26 years. Richard Middleton swallowed poison in Brussels at an age only a little more advanced. Both have been called geniuses, and undoubtedly *were* geniuses. But they were not geniuses because they committed suicide; which is to say, merely, that no such proof of their genius was required. Neither was loudly hailed as a genius, however, until he had destroyed himself. Without difficulty we may find in the work of both, evidences of a morbid wantonness that would make a bride of Death, particularly perhaps in the poetry of Middleton. If the fact may not be gainsaid, neither may it be exaggerated. The tales of Hubert Crackanthorpe and the sketches and poems of Richard Middleton, deeply as they are concerned often with the idea of death, obviously are the tales and poems of Youth, which ever is concerned with life's supreme mystery. Such evidences may be found in the writings of any person who ever has written; only we do not begin to look for them until a man has killed himself.

Hubert Crackanthorpe killed himself for love of a woman; Richard Middleton for loathing of life, the "intolerable evil" of which he was too conscious. Crackanthorpe, I am sure, loved life; Middleton, I think, hated it. Both died of their own wish and by their own deed. Crackanthorpe lived vividly, with a passionate interest in his fellow creatures; Middleton looked out of a win-

dow and dreamed fantastic dreams. Crackanthorpe, when he wrote, wrote of the lives he had
encountered about him and knew; of their little
joys and sorrows, their pride and their helpless-
ness, their egotism and their humility, and in
such detached, impersonal fashion that the irony
and terror of life was more realistically suggested by his stark, although impressionistic, reporting than any amount of comment could have
made it. Middleton remembered his childhood
and wove fancies out of old dreams, often very
happy ones indeed, bubbling with a whimsical
humor; but when he could not be a child, it was
of another existence he dreamed, and his lines
were sombre with the thought of death.

Crackanthorpe perhaps derives from Maupassant; Middleton almost certainly from Baudelaire. It will be recalled that Barbey d'Aurevilly
wrote to Baudelaire that the only thing for the
latter to do was to become a Christian or blow
out his brains. Crackanthorpe belonged to the
"eighteen-nineties," and Middleton to a somewhat later period, although Middleton reads
much like a *fin de siècle* "master," even more
so than Crackanthorpe; indeed he is somewhat of an anachronism. But this matter of
derivation and placing seems always an imper-
tinence to dwell upon, since we cannot know all

that has gone into the making of an artist, and classifying genius by periods is an extreme idiocy of pedantry.

I have used the word "reporting" in connection with the work of Crackanthorpe, and it may have been an unhappy word, for it inevitably suggests a gray picture of fact unrelieved by any touch of imagination. To suggest that of Crackanthorpe would be unfair, when evidences of his imaginative intelligence are to be found in almost any of his tales. What was meant is that in his careful and penetrating studies he is so concerned with the cruelty of life, with the emotional crises of human existence, that one can almost believe him to be chronicling experiences to which he was a witness, in which he was a participant. Youthful as is the cynicism of his uncompromising situations—his strongest book wears the terrible title, "Wreckage"—there is a maturity about his work that is little less than extraordinary. Richard Le Gallienne, who knew him, says that "hardly another writer of his generation had so thoroughly equipped himself for his calling of novelist by so adventurous a study of human life." I do not know exactly what that means, but even accepting it for what it would seem to mean, there must have been in Crackanthorpe's work much of what Henry James calls "anticipated experience"; and we can hardly deny imagination to a young man who, in his early twenties, could write "A Dead Woman." His was the gift of clairvoyance also vouchsafed Stephen Crane.

Had he lived, Hubert Crackanthorpe would have more than fulfilled his amazing promise. The "Set of Village Tales" at the end of his second volume ("Sentimental Studies"), and the "Vignettes" gathered into the little volume of that name, suggest powerfully the vivid impressionism toward which he was tending. These sad, glad little etchings in sunshine and in mist, for all their fragmentary appearance, are among his completest works.

In Middleton, the dreamer seemed ever to predominate, although often enough he managed to withhold the dream from his readers. But this is true only, I think, of his poetry, which is insignificant beside his prose. Life, for Richard Middleton, was a great mystery, not perhaps to be solved, but from little journeys toward the solution of which many half-revealed, supernal secrets might be glimpsed. Where Crackanthorpe was at his best in the episodic, concerned as *he* also was with the mystery of life, and relentlessly exposed his subjects in clinical detail, Middleton hovered on the borders of the occult, scorned anything like reality, and gave to his fancies the semblance of an allegory. *What does it all mean?* is his constant query; and, if he never answers the question, he furnishes significant clews, while over and through his tales there is a great light as of something ineffable about to be made known. There is much of what Arthur Machen calls "ecstasy" in his pages, notably in "The Ghost Ship," his finest production, and an indubitable masterpiece. Incidentally, Machen furnishes an introduction to the volume of that name, and I can think of no finer compliment to the memory of Richard Middleton than to say that Machen himself might have written the initial story. Poe, Stevenson, nor Ambrose Bierce need have taken shame to sign "The Coffin Merchant," nor Anatole France to attach his name to "The Soul of a Policeman."

Many of the tales in "The Ghost Ship" are, as I already have suggested, memories of childhood —amazingly remembered, superbly re-lived. "The Ghost Ship" will lead readers to "The Day Before Yesterday," a significant volume with a significant title, which contains much that is excellent, and so on to "Monologues," a final medley of periodical sketches, slighter than the others, but touched with the genius of a hunter after beauty who gave up the pursuit ere it was half run.

Crackanthorpe perished at 26; Middleton at 29. Crackanthorpe loved life passionately, and was fond of "healthy" adventure and sport in the open; Middleton, seeking the beauty he could not find, save as he could imagine it, came to loathe life, I think, and probably cared very little for what he would believe its superficial attractions and allurements. Each voluntarily relinquished the life he could no longer endure. Each is now called *genius,* and is busily "collected."

The person of sense, of course, knows perfectly well that these men did not prove their genius by their tragic self-effacement. It is none the less true that by calling attention to their genius in such shocking fashion a certain glamour has been added to their names, a certain piquant fascination to their work; and unthinking persons have not hesitated to connect the phenomenon with our earlier proposition. Hubert Crackanthorpe was no more mad than you who read, although one hesitates to assert that he was unvisited by a vision of fate. Richard Middleton, although his case is more complicated, certainly was no more mad than, let us say, I, who write— *Carpe diem, quam minimum credula postero!*—

since, reading him, I cry: "If this be madness, let us have less sanity!"

Many a man, I fancy, has killed himself because of a woman, who, had the pistol missed fire, or the rope broken, would have made no second attempt, but have gone on living quite sanely and quite thankfully for two deliverances; while if a thorough disgust with life as it is lived by the majority is a sign of insanity, I am personally acquainted with some dozens of apparently sane persons who are candidates for the asylum.

Hubert Crackanthorpe and Richard Middleton took their lives because, at the moment, they felt that they could no longer bear to go on living. That they sincerely believed this, is pitifully obvious. You may think Crackanthorpe foolish, if you wish to, but for him the death of Love was the end of all—at that moment, just before the plunge—and it is an emotion at which I do not care to sneer. But I am very sorry indeed. Middleton's death must have been, partially, in the nature of a protest, despite the beating wings that are heard in his poetry. I can think of nothing which conceivably might have eased Crackanthorpe; but Middleton's beautiful writings all were placed in covers *after* his death. . . Suppose someone had whispered a few words of sympathy and appreciation, and

it had been a bit less difficult for him to live and
write and sell his tales!

Or would either, had he lived, have written as
well again? It is a favorite notion that few men
are "called before their time"—or words to that
effect—that, at death, ordinarily, a writer has
done all that he would have done of any importance; has said, in effect, all that he had to say.
This strikes one as superstition and cant. If it
were sound even in theory, it is perfectly obvious
that many distinguished writers of this our little
day ought to have died years ago. Perhaps,
however, they are dead, and we have not yet
found it out; their publishers may be "holding
up their arms."

But need a writer die when he has written what
he had to write? When he has said what he had
to say? Why, for a time, should he not be allowed the happiness of some years of leisure as
a reward for his labors? . . Often, poor fellow, because the finer his product has been the
less it has brought him wherewith to finance a
trifle of leisure—always supposing him to be an
artist.

I don't know exactly what this paper proves,
whether it proves anything, or whether it is intended to prove anything. What it is, is a transcript of thoughts induced by listening to care-

less criticism and specious epigrams, and by reading the absurd comments of learned booksellers,
in catalogues of books that are rare and expensive
chiefly because they are beautiful and good.

THE IRRITATING MR. BURGESS

FEW authors make me angrier than Mr. Gelett Burgess. He is one of the most irritat-
ing persons now following the writing trade.
With the ability to do fine things, he persists in
writing quickly, carelessly, at times almost slov-
enly. It is an unpardonable thing in a man of
authentic talent.

Back in those glad, mad, bad, sad days of the
eighteen-nineties, Mr. Burgess was ring-leader in
a literary renaissance on this side of the Atlantic
that all but paralleled the glittering pageant in
Europe. As one of the editors of *The Lark*
(poor Doxey, who published it, died only a short
time ago), put forth by *les jeunes* of San Francisco, then the American Bagdad, he produced a
quality of improbable fiction that had much of
the charm of, and was confessedly patterned after, Stevenson's "New Arabian Nights." He
wrote quantities of sparkling verse in the French
forms (since collected in a delightful volume
called "A Gauge of Youth") and disclosed a
fancy as vivacious and unbridled as the Parisians.
In practically every department of literary endeavor, he cut grotesque capers with twinkling
heels, carrying off everything with an air of in-
souciance that was irresistible.

Gone with his youth, I fear, are these delightful pleasantries.

There is nothing timely about this paper. No
new Burgess volume has come from the press to
tempt these sad recollections of other days; the
latest, I believe, is some years of age and was—
alas!—something of a "best seller." And yet, it
is the later works of this author that prompt
these remarks; I have been looking them over
and thinking how good they might have been!

Take, for instance, his cyclical novel—cyclical
isn't quite the word, but it will do—"Find the
Woman." There is a book so nearly good that it
almost moves one to tears in the realization there-
of. As in the tales of the Cigar Divan, one
progressive narration is achieved through the telling of a number of sprightly *contes,* each complete enough in itself and yet each hinging definitely upon the other for the ultimate *dènouement.* There are flights of fancy in it that
suggest the Burgess of old, the immortal Gelett
who wrote "Vivette" (acquit me, please, of an
intentional rhyme), and humorous touches that
tickle the risibilities to ecstasy. Who but Burgess, for example, could achieve so whimsical a
conceit as that of the colored boy at the helm of
the apartment building "lift," reading "Middle-

march" and laying it reluctantly aside to waft his
passengers to the upper floors?

There are at least a dozen flashes just an inimitable, and some of the incidental tales are excellent, but for the most part the humor is of
the slangy sort and therefore a bit cheap. Why
should Mr. Burgess employ slang at all? The
fact that it is in general use these sordid days is
no reason, for this is no more a modern book
than is "Don Quixote" or "The Thousand and
One Nights." It is modern only in its chrono-
logical and geographical features; change the
names, dates and places and the tale is mediæval
—as it should be. Stevenson, too, employed modern settings, but the tone of his writing (in his
Arabian paraphrases) is thoroughly antique; his
Smiths and *Joneses* are *Husseins* or *Dom Pedros*
in frock coats and silk tiles, their conversation no
more the talk of the hour than the Songs of Solo-
mon.

In a book of this sort it is a mistake for characters to talk as they do in life; the book becomes
a paradox. The story is thoroughly, charmingly
unreal to begin with—no one would have it otherwise—and touches actual conditions seldom indeed, and then only to satirize and caricature.
Why, then, make the persons of the play living
persons? In the books of Theodore Dreiser peo-

ple are "peepul," and there is no fault to be found on that score; in the holiday performances of Stevenson (the most typical man in the field under discussion) they are—and where they are not, they should be—shadows, marionettes, uttering perfumed phrases and specious epigrams at every tug at the wire. Where the charm of a story is its unreality, the perfection of unreality would seem to be the highest art.

We have come a long way from "Find the Woman," perhaps. It is hardly deserving of too serious consideration, eminently readable though it is. The point is, if Mr. Gelett Burgess had cared to give a year to its manufacture, instead of—as I suspect—a couple of months, it would have been a better book, more deserving of an accusation of derivation from its greater brethren, the "New Arabian Nights," "The Dynamiter," and Machen's "The Three Imposters."

Even "Vivette" did not quite stack up with Stevenson, of course, but it was a diverting and amusing echo, unashamedly imitative and dedicated, indeed, to Mrs. R. L. S., then living in or near California and worshipped by *les jeunes*. The sub-title of the little book (now at a premium) reads as follows: "The Memoirs of the Romance Association: Setting forth the diverting Adventures of one Richard Redforth in the very pleasant City of Millamours: how he took Service in the Association: how he met and wooed the gay Vivette: how they sped their Honeymoon and played the Town: how they spread a mad Banquet, of them that came thereto and the Tales they told: of the Exploits of the principal Characters, and especially of the Disappearance of Vivette." I defy anyone to read that and then not want to read the book.

It was the maddest thing imaginable, as mad and irresponsible as a kitten or a mountain stream; as mad and irresponsible as the moment in literary history that gave it birth, the *fin de siècle* renaissance (or decadence, as you please) that turned England, France and America into a three-ring literary circus to the tune of "Ta-ra-ra-boom-de-ay!"

"I doubt if ever I have recaptured that first, fine, careless rapture of youth," wrote Burgess about this book, or words to that effect. It is true, but he has come so almighty close on one or two other occasions that I, for one, choose to be angry about it.

In collaboration with Will Irwin, another Californian, Burgess wrote two books in the same picaresque vain. Neither was as good as "Vivette;" both were better, I think, than "Find the Woman." But in "Find the Woman," Burgess, without a collaborator, came nearer to rewriting "Vivette," for although he failed he seemed more in the swing and lilt of the thing. "The Reign of Queen Isyl" and "The Picaroons" are better, but the vein is not quite the same. In "The Picaroons," in particular, the modernity of the dialogue is more permissible (slang is all right in its place), and "The Reign of Queen Isyl" really is more of a New Orleans *mardi gras* than it is a sixteenth century pageant.

Too, in a book called "Lady Mechante," Burgess aims at his early standard, and in a volume of whimsical essays entitled "The Romance of the Commonplace." He is only fairly successful; in both cases one has the feeling that the author has lost something that he is striving to regain. The "something," of course, is that "first careless rapture" to which Burgess refers. . .

Discussion of his entertaining nonsense books (he is the creator of the "Goops") and his contributions to our American vocabulary in "Are You a Bromide?" is outside the province of this paper. They neither add to nor subtract from his stature.

Perhaps it is unfair to expect a man to repeat his finest performance, or—arresting thought!— perhaps it is I who have lost that early rapture. Perhaps it is still in Burgess's pages and I, grown old in wickedness and Anatole France, fail to find it! But no, I have his own confession; and I have seen his very latest works—"The White Cat," and other popular novels of the "best seller order. Let us be grateful, at any rate, for what we have; for Burgess's realization of his failings. Even at his worst, he is frequently head and shoulders above the average entertainer.

But, as I have suggested, few authors make me angrier than Mr. Gelett Burgess.

OPIE READ AND THE
GREAT AMERICAN NOVEL

"THE greatest almoster this country ever produced," cried the editor of *Reedy's Mirror* enthusiastically when I suggested a paper on Opie Read—summing up in a phrase what I had planned to say in perhaps a column or two. That thought was to have been my introduction and my epilogue, for while it is the obvious remark it is also the inevitable word. In the circumstances, bereft of my text, I must credit it to its author and still use it.

Somehow, I cannot think of Opie Read without thinking also of that literary will-o'-the-wisp, the Great American Novel. Let it be said at once that Opie didn't write it, grotesquely supposing it to have been written, and couldn't write it, optimistically supposing it may yet be done. Opie Read is provincial, and the Great American Novel cannot be that. What Opie Read might have done—what he almost did do—is write great American novels.

This thought about the Great American Novel obtrudes because there have been so few American novels which, by any manner of reasoning, might be entered for that handicap, and because Opie's are so entirely American. Yet in that brief muster of thoroughbreds, at least six of Opie Read's novels would have to be started. The G. A. N.—it has come to be initialed, like G. B. S. and other myths—*never will* be written, in point of fact. Spain alone, of all nations, may claim an unique book: and who is to say what the future shall bring out of Spain?

Opie Read is of the line of Shakespeare and Dickens, as was Mark Twain. Removed from its context that line would seem a staggering absurdity. Opie's wildest admirer might hesitate to say that, at his best, Opie approximated those others at their worst. Actually, he is not—so—very—far—behind Dickens and St. Mark, if we except the outstanding master-works of that excellent pair. The point is, all were elemental geniuses who, whatever we may think of their work as "art," in our current cant, had (1) a story to tell, and (2) told it. We may speak of Opie in the past tense for critical purposes, for he is through with novel writing. Shakespeare and Dickens and Mark Twain wrote about "peepul," even when the former was writing about Earls and Ladies; and about life as it is lived, and about human emotions. Lacking the superior genius of these, but spurred by a curious genius

of his own, of a less distinguished fervor, Opie
Read wrote too of "peepul" and life, as he had
observed them, and like those others his first consideration was his story, the thing he had to say
rather than the technical consideration of style.
Opie himself called Shakespeare "the Bible's wise
though sometimes sportive child," so I must not
insist too hard on this Shakespeare analogy lest
my reward be laughter; but I may continue to
this: like those others, also, when in the course
of Opie's narrative the English language threat-
ened to obstruct the flow of his thought, it was the
English language that suffered. It went by the
board, and Opie wrote copiously without reference to such minutiae as the rules governing our
parts of speech and their "proper" juxtaposition.
Only a courageous genius or a fool may do this
successfully, and Opie Read was—and is—no
fool.

This is not to say that Opie Read's writings
do not possess style. Out of his fine scorn for
dilettante word painting achieved at the expense
of philosophical content, he accomplished a clear,
expressive and often highly poetic manner; but
he is no more a stylist than is Dickens or Balzac.
The great Frenchman is another whom, remotely,
he suggests. The *thing* in Opie Read is his profound knowledge of human nature, his cheerful

and whimsical philosophy, the rugged virility of his democracy. A novelist with a purpose, he believes in human nature, sees the good in the bad and the bad in the good, and draws no false distinctions among men. In his philosophy one class does not possess all the virtues and another all the faults of humanity. He sees life as he sees nature, with the understanding eye and the sympathetic heart. He is not a mystic; neither, however, is he a materialist nor a sensationalist. I think of him as that rare and joyous anomaly— an artist who is perfectly disillusioned, and is still an optimist.

I have said that Opie Read is provincial, and so he is—geographically. The passions of his middle west and southern characters are, of course, common from China to Peru—with such variations as may be developed by the gulf stream and Governmental idiocy. I am of those, how- ever, who believe with Machen and Cabell that great literature must be allegorical rather than locally descriptive; and while Opie is a writer of allegories in that, unobtrusively, his tales point an admirable moral, he is none the less confined within the frontiers of three or four states, and tied to the native peculiarities and endeavors of citizens indigenous to the locale of his scenario. With this restriction, his imagination voyages bravely with his experience, and a veritable *Comedic Humaino,* somewhat liquid and drawling as to speech, is the result.

Something of a *picaro* himself, Read's wandering heroes are often picturesquely picaresque vagabonds of the genus printer. Opie was a printer in his youth, and the "tramp printer," that inspired scare-crow beloved of Mark Twain and earlier humorists, is intimately known to him. Whatever else his tales may be about, Opie usually manages to drag in a printer, and he makes of him an ingratiating and thoroughly likable hero-villain—brilliant, temperamental, entirely undependable and perennially drunk. Perhaps I exaggerate here, very slightly, just as Opie doubtless exaggerates and caricatures his man; but I insist that his printers are chock full of human frailties, and, by the same token, entirely human and delightful.

But it was a lawyer who in that (to me) most charming of his yarns, "The Wives of the Prophet," carried on scandalously in a religious community, where, as a matter of rite, tri-annually the loveliest girls were set aside to be the "wives of the prophet." The prophet never had been known to come; the lovely maidens later became wives or old maids, languished and died; but while they lived they never ceased to tell of the

honor that had been theirs. It was a signal compliment thus to be "set aside" to await the coming
of the "prophet." All of which coming to the
ears of Opie's vagabond, inflamed him to high
resolve—and one day the "prophet" came.   O
lovers of the mad *Don Q.*, of *Gil Blas* and *Guzman de Alfarache,* of Laurence Sterne and the
redoubtable *Pickwick*—read you the story! It is,
I suppose, leagues behind the world masterpieces,
but it is of their lively kidney.

For the most part, Opie Read is known for "A
Kentucky Colonel," "A Tennessee Judge," "An
Arkansas Planter," "Emmet Bonlore," "The
Jucklins" and a dozen other minor masterpieces
of American community life. His Southern colo-
nels and judges, and their devoted darkies, are
lovingly and tenderly drawn by a man who knew
and called them by their names—"Kernel" and
"Jedge" and "Joe." Their quaint philosophies,
their shrewd wit, their camaraderie, their chivalry,
their weaknesses and their strength, are all in
the books. Opie has idealized them, he has even
been a bit maudlin about it at times; but allowing for caricature, kindly or indignant (and Read
is a vigorous denouncer, too), these are the *men.*
In "My Young Master" he has written as fine
a novel of the civil war as our literature can offer,
and in "Bolanyo" he has focused a community so

sharply as to deceive one into a belief that perhaps the book is even finer than it seems. But in
"Bolanyo" he fails where in many of his other
tales he manages to fail; he is in too big a hurry.
Toward the end he lets down; he is writing too
furiously—not with the fury of composition, but
with the fury of imperative haste.

Therein is found one reason why Opie Read is
not one of the great novelists. I don't know
what his ambition may have been as a young
man, though it must have been high; but for one
reason or another he had to write rapidly for a
peculiar market. His popularity with the traveling public was enormous, and his publishers were
in the business of issuing paper-backed novels in
astonishing quantities, at incredible speed. I
fancy Opie was usually behind on his contracts.
I can imagine his publishers frantically querying
him concerning a book supposed to be nearing
completion and actually not yet begun. I can
imagine Opie buying a basket of stogies, a pound
of pipe tobacco and a bottle of ink out of the
miserable remnants of his advance money and
plunging to the task. But once begun I do not
see him tearing his hair and gesticulating. The
born story-teller is at work now; the teeming
fancy is leaps ahead of the coursing pen, and
without the remotest idea of what is coming next

in the story Opie is turning out wet pages at a
rate that Walter Scott, writing to pay his debts,
might have envied. So it must have been at any
rate toward the last. That it was always so one
might do him an injustice to guess. He himself
has said: "There is no genius except it be whole-
souled desire and persistent effort. The genius
works late. When he goes to bed the oil in his
lamp is low. He sometimes works with the energy of despair, and at last sees success through
a mist of tears."

Did he ever correct any of his manuscripts?
Possibly he did—in his early days, perhaps. They
wouldn't need much correcting, for he was not
the sort to blunder badly. And first thoughts
usually are best, if a man is not consciously striving for style; but writing at a gallop is dangerous for the best of men, unless one intends at
least to read over what he has written, and knows
as he writes what the next chapter is to contain.
The wonder is that Opie Read wrote as well as
he did; the pity is that he did not write as he
could have written.

His humor and his philosophy went hand in
hand. As a random sample of his style, in this
connection, perhaps the following is adequate:
"Man may be walking pleasantly with Prosperity
hooked upon his arm, talking of the deeds they

are to perform in common, when up gallops
Misfortune on a horse, and that is the end." Or
this bit of blithe cynicism: "The ancient philoso-
phers, counseling contentment of the mind, had
money loaned out at interest. It was no wonder
that they could be contented, and, after all, they
held the right idea of life: money first and philosophy afterward." His epigrams are as clever
as those turned by weightier names. "Marriage,"
he remarks in one book, "is a noisy failure or a
quiet blessing"; and, "One may have ever so
hairy an ear, and yet the gossip of the neighborhood will force its way in." His humor usually
is homespun; it doesn't glitter. And at his worst,
when he moralizes, Read never offends with the
awful "glad" philosophy of certain popular writers of the week.

Opie himself is a character out of his own
books. He is a physical giant, or he would not
now be living. At the Chicago Press Club,
which is his headquarters, he is the sole survivor
of a brilliant group that once included Stanley
Waterloo, H. S. Canfield and John McGovern
—excellent writers and splendid fellows, in no
small degree wrecked by a harlot city. He is the
"show piece" of that newspaper institution, and
occasionally graces a banquet with his long presence and an humorous speech—a "speech" al-

ways; he never makes addresses. He is as good an extemporaneous speaker as ever was inveigled into sudden articulation.

As a young reporter I used to frequent the Chicago Press Club, usually to steal a nap on one of its sofas. Not infrequently I was awakened by a booming voice lambasting life, letters and all the powers that be. Sleepily, I knew that Opie had come in, and was in his favorite chair. I did not always listen; I wish now that I had. But thinking back and looking forward, I incline to believe that some day there may be readers who will envy that obscure journalist, if happily they chance upon his tribute, who lay sometimes upon a hair sofa and listened idly to tales more remarkable than their author ever spun in print.

A BOOKMAN OF THE OLD SCHOOL

F EW men of our time so well have exemplified
the literary tradition as Walter Blackburn
Harte—the old literary tradition, of course, of
Lamb, De Quincey, Hazlitt, and Gissing. I
think of Harte as an immortal hack, harassed
and driven, alternately gay and despondent as his
fortunes waxed and waned, impecunious ever
and often hungry, climbing long, creaking stairs
to his garret under the eaves, and there, at length,
in obscurity, dying, with the taunting reminders
of his first and only published volume about him.
Yet that is not an entirely accurate picture—it is
the way I see and think of him. But the true picture, alas, varies only in detail and is no whit happier, for Harte was in truth a newspaper hack,
impecunious, harassed and driven, and a large
remnant of his only volume, "Meditations in Motley," kept him companion for years in his attic.
Whether he died there, I do not know; but he
died young and tragically of disease, having
wrecked his health in a service he loathed, and his
life, in a measure, by his uncompromising loyalty
to his ideals. He died of journalism, say his
friends, and there is much to support the state-

ment. His "Meditations," a small volume dated
1894, never brought him a penny, although it is
one of the comparatively few specimens in authentic *belles-lettres* in our recent literature. He
dedicated it, by the way, to "The Devil and Dame
Chance, the two most potent deities in literary
fortunes as in all other sublunary dispensations."
And as his friend Percival Pollard said "that bit
of truth-telling was never forgiven him by either."

Harte had no talent for success, little talent
indeed for happiness, as the word usually is understood. He was a bookman of an old school,
and from the seclusion of his attic he sent forth
lightning flashes of condemnation, of caustic dis-
approval of the literature and life of his day, not
at all calculated to increase his popularity among
those who published bad books, bad newspapers,
or their own stupidity by word of mouth. Such
masterly essays in repressed invective as "Ja-
cobitism in Boston," "About Critics and Criticism," and "Some Masks and Faces of Literature," proved his honesty, his critical acumen and
his strength; but naturally enough they made
him few friends. The inevitable conspiracy of
silence was formed against him, and he was forced
to publish where he could and as he might. For
this reason, much of his best work still lies buried

in the files of long-dead journals, and Walter
Blackburn Harte is a name seldom spoken and
all but unknown.

Here are a few typical, and by no means un-
timely examples of his style and thought, selected
quite at random:

> The worst of being a professional literary critic is
> that you are brought into collision with so many fools
> every week—in gilt edges, cloth and paper covers. A
> man had far better ruin his palate as a tea-taster than
> poison the sources of his imagination and inner life
> as a literary taster. . . .
>
> There are some preternaturally dull big-wigs, of
> very high standing in the literary world, who write as
> if they were muffled up in the shrouds of dead authors.
> They are ashamed of nature, and are as dependent
> upon precedent as police magistrates. They dare not
> look up and see God's sun shining in the heavens, un-
> less some illustrious predecessor in their libraries has
> already made note of the phenomenon. They are
> afraid to compromise the dignity of the fancy figures
> they conjure up in their minds, of themselves, for the
> delectation of posterity. This is the only matter in
> which such men betray the smallest possession of
> imagination: they can see nothing worthy or beautiful
> in their own generation, but they are greatly concerned
> to impress a proper sense of their personal dignity and
> talents upon the hopeful children of their worthless
> contemporaries—if not upon those lost souls them-
> selves. They despise their contemporaries so much,
> because, while looking back, they also look forward,
> and fancy they belong to no generation but to pos-
> terity. . . .
>
> The newspapers and their peculiar intellectual and
> moral methods and influences are indisputable facts;

and the immense prosperity of the newspapers, at the
cost of the dwarfed mental and moral perceptions of
the masses, is, perhaps, the most portentous fact of
this century; and, therefore, the doctrine of total depravity is removed from the perplexed region of theology and is proved beyond all question. . . .

The biographical dictionary of American authors,
with a few conspicuous exceptions, is more than anything else a record of poor devils whose talents were
wholly perverted, and whose lives were wrecked, by
the accident of having been born into the wrong hemis-
phere. . . .

But Harte also sent forth from his attic some
of the most perfect philosophical essays we have
had—essays that read well, indeed, beside those
of Montaigne and Stevenson, and that, occasionally, have more than a passing flavor of the old-
fashioned "Autocrat." Might not the following,
for instance, be set down almost anywhere in
Dr. Holmes's volume, and merge pleasantly
into the context? It is the opening paragraph in
Harte's essay "On Certain Satisfactions of Prejudice."

Over a cup of tea and the evening paper I am
constantly informed by the delightful old lady, who
sits at the end of the board and gravely and quietly
replenishes my cup without any demur until the limit
of five cups is reached, when neither prayers, threats
nor entreaties will induce her to pour out another drop,
that I am a person of violent antipathies and prejudices. When I attempt to remonstrate and clear my-

self of this dreadful charge, by explaining that any splenetic explosions in which I may occasionally indulge at the table are imbued with the high moral purpose of shaking the company out of their immoral apathy, I only make matters worse.

That is the leisurely manner of the ancients, or, at least, of the Victorians, and it is a manner that has all but vanished from the earth, to the regret of the present writer if of none other.

And so the world would have none of Walter Harte, or, perhaps, it is truer to say that the world had no particular opportunity either to accept or reject him. There was no subserviency in him, and he knew nothing of compromise; he flatly refused to adapt himself. His courage was immense, but it was greater than his strength. He stooped to journalism, which he hated, and it killed him with neatness and dispatch. That was perhaps the only concession he ever made, and, as he might have said himself, he paid for it. A brilliant failure, he fought his losing fight for a time, and finally—he died.

From all this, one might suppose him to be the sort of genius who, bitter and frustrated, takes his own life, but one would be wrong. For one thing, he found a considerable happiness in his books. This passion for books has made life endurable to others than Walter Blackburn

Harte. Undoubtedly, too, it influenced his style, and to some extent his thought. As a writer of sparkling and suggestive prose, he had, in his day, few superiors, and his manner is none the less his own because sometimes it suggests another. His didacticism, perhaps, suggests Addison, and his irony Thackeray, and it may be regarded as certain that he knew Addison and Thackeray as well as he knew Stevenson and Lamb.

Harte was for some years assistant editor of the *New England Magazine,* and many of his finest essays were written for that journal, and printed in his department, "In a Corner at Dodsley's." From thence he passed to the *Arena,* and eventually he joined the pamphlet movement with a little venture of his own—the *Fly-Leaf.* He found his greatest happiness in this tiny journal, and for a while it promised success, but Harte's credulity wrecked him; he allowed himself to be persuaded by Elbert Hubbard to incorporate the *Fly-Leaf* with the *Philistine,* and the partnership was about as happy as might have been expected. It lasted eighteen days. When it ended, the *Fly-Leaf* was dead and Harte took to reporting.

Something of his feelings at this time may be understood in the light of a letter to his friend, Percival Pollard, in which he wrote:

I am alive—but if I were more of an idealist, and more of a philosopher at that, I should affirm at the same time that I am dead. Morally, at any rate, I am dead and buried. I am earning my bread and butter as a newspaper brigand. This, in America, is about the worst possible pass any man with any refinement of character, and any moral feeling can come to. I have no sympathy at all with hustle and noise and the triumph of machinery or of democracy as we get it, with Tammany and the hoodlums on top in society, politics and literature. I regard this democracy as a governing power, especially in all intellectual matters, as the worst possible catastrophe. The mob from the time of Socrates until to-day has been governed by its belly and its vanity and brutal passions, and politically and socially needs the constant crack of the whips about its ears, in order to keep accord with the scheme of Nature—grovelling on its belly!

. . . Every writer ought to put away all belief in the mob—it is the wanton that destroys us from a mere whim of total depravity. The mob! how many lives are ruined and have been ruined in America by the mob! What a pity George Washington was not made an absolute monarch with a conscience to teach the whelps good manners, and to give the arts the sanction of the only thing the mob respects, the sanction of the interest of the accidentally great ones of the earth.

It is easy to think that, in a sense, Harte's failure, his misery, his death, was his own fault; but in a much larger sense nothing could be farther from the truth. He *was* hardly used. Is a man his own worst enemy when he fights a courageous and honest battle against hypocrisy and stupidity, when the odds are fearfully against him?

HALDANE MACFALL, NOVELIST

I SAY novelist, because, save to the intimate minority, Haldane Macfall's reputation in the past largely has rested upon his critical writings. As an art critic, he is something of a power in London, and I think something of a terror, too, to poseurs and claquers. During the war he gained a wide audience with two books explaining the horror to the Man-in-the-street, for he is also a practical soldier of long experience, and is entitled to call himself Major. Meanwhile, his novels languish, and it is primarily as a novelist that Haldane Macfall will figure in the literary chronicles of the future.

Mr. Macfall will write other novels before he dies, but he need not unless he wishes. His fame is assured by those already written: "The Wooings of Jezebel Pettyfer" and "The Masterfolk." Few better novels have been written in the language.

Before I go farther, I must acknowledge my indebtedness to Judge Malmin. Loitering in Walter Hill's book shop, upon a day, I was beset by an excited man who plunged in, awkwardly waving a book about his head. The man was Lucius J. M. Malmin, chief justice of the Virgin

Islands, and America's first colonial judge; the book was "The Wooings of Jezebel Pettyfer." The man had found the book in a shop in St. Thomas, an island recently purchased from Denmark. With some agitation, he handed me the volume, saying: "I'm afraid to say what I think about this book. I've brought it up from St. Thomas for you to read. I know it isn't famous, but either I'm crazy or this is one of the great books of the world!"

Obeisance to Judge Malmin. The next day, I was as excited as he. I sat up all night to finish the book's 403 pages, breakfasting on strong coffee at five o'clock. Then I wrote to Haldane Macfall. A little later, I read "The Masterfolk," and now I am trying to excite others. If I am fortunate, I shall always marvel at the odd chance that brought *Jezebel Pettyfer* up from the Virgin Islands (a strange place for Jezebel!) to my Chicago apartment, and whatever may happen I shall always be grateful to Judge Malmin—and, of course, to Haldane Macfall.

The habit of comparing one book with another, of allowing it to stand or fall, critically, by its measure as taken beside that of a classic, is a vicious one; but remotely to suggest the charm and flavor of "The Wooings of Jezebel Petty-

fer," I am going to say that it is a West Indian
blend of *Pickwick, The Three Musketeers,* and
the Spanish romances of roguery. I shall not
push the comparison, although certainly Macfall
is of the line of the great romancers.

Jezebel Pettyfer is a Barbadian negress, utterly reckless, unmoral and delightful. Even more
adjectival are Jehu Sennacherib Dyle, her first
recorded lover, and his amazing companions.
Around this yellow pair, and its satellites, cen-
ters the long and rambling narrative of West
Indian life. . . Deserted by his mother, "Ma-
sheen" Dyle (as he comes to be known, through
his theft of a sewing machine) is thrown upon
his small world of dirt and color at the age of
nine, and manages to pry open the oyster in a
fashion worthy the traditions of *Lazarillo de
Tormes* and *Guzman de Alfarache.* Untruth-
ful, unscrupulous, unblushing, the saffron *picaro*
progresses through vagabond youth to disreputable middle life, as barrack boy, butler, soldier,
deserter and fugitive, and the successive love
affairs of Jezebel Pettyfer keep step with his
astonishing adventures.

There is no more plot to the book than there is
to "Tristram Shandy," and that is one reason
that it is great. The other reasons have to do with
Mr. Macfall's uncensored and uproarious humor,

his fine humanity and tolerance, and the tumult
and gusto of his style—some would call it his
lack of style. The vigor of the narrative is extraordinary, and the characterization unforgettable. Dyle, Jezebel, Boaz Bryan and the rest of
the sable company remain in the memory as do
Sam Weller and *Huck Finn*—sometimes, as do
Pantagruel and *Panurge*. The chapter in which
Huckleback, the Jamaican inn keeper, is killed
by the English sailor, is one of the great scenes
in English fiction, but there are other chapters
almost equally good, and the purely descriptive
passages are gorgeous revelations.

Ten books, or divisions, complete the narrative;
and a very remarkable series of chapters makes
up the book called "In the House of the Sorcerer." In this there is an appalling description of
West Indian voodoo. If any fuller revelation of
the obscene mysteries of voodoo has been vouchsafed in print, I have not seen it. . . It should
be mentioned, here, that these particular chapters
once were published in this country under the
title, "The House of the Sorcerer," but that book
is less than one half of the full tale, and is now
out of print.

That all this praise should be given a novel of
negro life may seem strange, although why it
should, I do not know; the novel is an authentic

masterpiece, possibly the last of the great line of picaresque romances which began with "Lazarillo de Tormes" and includes "Tyl Eulenspigel," "Gil Blas," and the "Pickwick Papers." There is all the freedom, all the roguery, all the romance, and all the rollicking, ironic philosophy of the best of them, and "Jezebel Pettyfer" is as deserving of immortality as any.

I have been looking over some of the old "notices" of the novel, the trumpetings and shudderings of the reviewers of 1898. The book made a sensation. Coming as it did at the height of the "renaissance of the nineties," it must have frightened some of the posing critics of that period half to death. The sickly imaginings of the English decadents must have seemed pale stuff beside the broad fun of Jehu Dyle and his nigger Zouaves. Afraid to damn the book, many reviewers avoided the issue of greatness by ambiguous platitudes, but many, too, were outspoken in its favor, and frankly called it great. That it bothered the critics mightily is very evident. Old George Meredith enigmatically told the author that the book was the finest novel of his generation, but that it ought never to have been written!

The strangest feature of the case is that the great book was allowed to go out of print. In the midst of the shout, a fire in the publisher's plant destroyed what remained of the edition, and he refused to reprint. It was not until 1913 that a second edition was placed on the market. Copies of this, I am happy to report, are still to be procured; and it is pleasant to know that the reissue was brought about by hundreds of requests from all parts of the world—isolated requests in themselves, but constituting a formidable demand when assembled in the publisher's office.

It is a long time since I have been as enthusiastic about a book as I am about "Jezebel Pettyfer," for it is a long time since I have found anything new in this genre. Here is the stuff of Rabelais and Grimmelshausen, of Le Sage and Sterne, geographically translated to the tropics; and the author still lives and writes. The book is of our own day, yet is neither translation nor redaction; but it is of the shining company. This may seem incredible, but it is true.

In "The Masterfolk," which is dedicated to Meredith, Mr. Macfall writes of literary London and artist Paris in the eighteen-nineties, and some of his maskers are thinly disguised. Like its predecessor, this novel appeared in America, some years ago, sadly cropped and abbreviated. To read it in its entirety, it is necessary to procure the London edition.

I am enthusiastic about "The Masterfolk," too, but in a different way. This novel belongs to another school. It is a great novel in the sense that "David Copperfield" and "Joseph Vance" are great novels; a full and generous account of the career of its chief figure from a point just this side of the womb to the birth of the hero's own first child. It is concerned almost exclusively with the bohemian life, and is a first-hand chronicle of an arresting period in literature.

There have been other novels concerned with the eighteen-nineties, in which the decadents were glorified; this, in large part, is the other side of the episode. The specious philosophy of the great poseurs of the age is reduced to rags and tatters, and a number of eminent reputations still beloved of collectors of first editions (I am convinced that I could give the real names of half the characters in the book), are made extremely ludicrous and contemptible by the author's biting satire. Hichens' "The Green Carnation" has been widely accepted as the crowning satire on *fin de siècle* London, but, as Mr. Holbrook Jackson has pointed out, that ingenious work is in reality less of a satire than an indiscretion; at any rate, it was a *tour de force*. For me, "The Masterfolk" is the last word on the English decadents.

Also, I think it contains the best pictures of student life in Paris that I have read.

The story is that of Noll Baddlesmere and Betty Modeyne, and the numerous company with which their fortunes were cast. I shall now proceed to damn the book for a great many sonorous donkeys by saying that, in spots, it is highly Dickensian. It is the fashion, now, to sneer at Dickens —not that Dickens cares! Yes, the tale is romantic to a degree. More, it is often sentimental. *Mon Dieu!* Poor Mr. Macfall! But sneers from sonorous donkeys are praise indeed, and so we may continue happily with the story. I was going to say that the tale is intensely human, in that it is humorous and humane, ironic and compassionate. To make it completely great, there is that touch of caricature and exaggeration that should accompany romance in a tale not of the immediate present. Having read this novel, one has made the acquaintance of a company of persons from whom never again is one quite willing to be parted. Drawn full length, for Mr. Macfall is always outspoken, his familiars live with the other memorable figures with whom the great novelists have peopled the world for our delight.

To complete the bibliography, I must mention a third essay in fiction—like the others it is colored truth—execrably entitled "The Nut in War."

Mr. Macfall's title, "The Unlicked Cub," is retained as a sub-title, but his publisher played to the gallery. It is a short story of novelette length, and relates the experiences of a "nut" (English, not American, idiom) in a hectic African campaign. The tale is vivid and entertaining, but to speak of it beside the two novels is to flatter it.

Lest the tone of this paper offend, I hasten to add that it is no shout of discovery. Others have discovered Haldane Macfall; he is being discovered every few years, and with each discovery a new shout goes up. And with each shout fresh readers are won to this fine novelist. But the clamor has been too isolated and sporadic. If it can be made sustained, perhaps in time it will reach an attuned ear in the American publishing world.

ROBERT NEILSON STEPHENS AND
THE COSTUME NOVEL

THE day before yesterday always has been a glamor day. The present is sordid and prosaic. Time colors history as it does a meerschaum pipe. The sweet days of old are little vignettes of vanished happinesses quaintly preserved in little silver frames. Is it not so?

Fictional narratives centering about an early day (in America, the Revolutionary period, let us say) are romantic to a degree; reading them we sigh for that perished splendor. Yet we may be sure that our grandsires, and their grandsires, too, turned back with captured eyes to the "good old days" of still earlier generations.

The thought is not particularly new, and in the red light of the late war it may seem less true now than before those fires were kindled; but the "romance" of the world war has not yet operated to soften the outlines of horror. And the thought is still sufficiently new to furnish a text for a discussion of the popularity of historical fiction.

The tendency of the day, in serious letters, is toward realistic fiction and contemporaneous

179

manners; but publishers still bring forth, now
and again, specimens of the cloak and sword
drama that we associate with other years—almost
with vanished races. It may be assumed that
they do so because those dashing chronicles find
readers enow to warrant the venture. It is well
that this is so. As on the stage, from time to
time, occur revivals of old favorite types, the
costume drama and the "island comedy," so it is
with books—the echo of clinking swords and the
clatter of horses' hoofs never entirely dies in the
distance. The wheel turns, time passes, and after
a while the romantic drama of personal adventure again is uppermost.

When such a renaissance comes to pass, the
writer who best achieves that glamor of reality
that is the soul of historical romance, is the writer most likely to engage our affection. James
Branch Cabell has pointed out that "first-class art
never reproduces its surroundings," and while at
rare intervals some genius arises to confound this
dictum, it is still perilously near to being a rule.

The late Robert Neilson Stephens (How his
name reminds one of a greater Robert!), without
being a writer of the first rank, was an entertainer of considerable fascination, who in an unusual degree possessed the power to reconstruct
and color old epochs. Two things prevented his

reaching full stature: his prolificacy and his early
death. But in his day (he died in 1906, *aetat* 38)
he commanded a large and enthusiastic audience, and one at least of his romances was made
into a drama of consummate beauty.

Stephens' most popular book, perhaps, was
"An Enemy to the King," which was dramatized
for Sothern and produced with remarkable success. His best book, in my opinion, was—and
is—"Captain Ravenshaw," an Elizabethan narrative in which Shakespeare's London is recovered and presented as seldom elsewhere in recent
fiction have I encountered it and felt its spell.
From the first engaging adventure of the capti-
vating ruffian Ravenshaw—a sort of Villon of
the period—to the concluding chapter, it is a
gorgeous chronicle of a day than which there is
none more alluring in history. It was Stephens'
most elaborate and painstaking venture, in prep-
aration for which he spent months in the English
capital, and more months in bookish research; and
as it was his last completed novel, we may find in
it justifiable evidence that its author was looking
steadily upward. Lovers of the man from Strat-
ford, and his now almost mythical time, who are
unfamiliar with *Captain Ravenshaw,* should
make the acquaintance of this Elizabethan soldier
of fortune, who was not unknown to Master Will

and Rare Ben Jonson, and whose truculent hulk darkened the Mermaid doors more often than the landlord cared to remember.

In an earlier romance, "A Gentleman Player," Stephens had evidenced his fondness for Shakespeare's England, and produced an excellent story; but it is not as good a tale as "Captain Ravenshaw," a fact that perhaps its author recognized when he began to think about the latter book. "A Gentleman Player" is concerned with the misadventures of a company of strolling players of the period and, in particular, those of a young play-actor whose lovemaking was not of the smoothest. Shakespeare himself figures in the narrative.

In "An Enemy to the King" and "A Dash to Paris" there is the flavour, without the crowded incident and boisterous charm, of the D'Artagnan romances. They may have been, and possibly were influenced by Dumas, and while they are *not* Dumas they are still admirable stories, swiftly and vividly told. As in "Ravenshaw" and the "Gentleman Player," the outstanding figures are venturesome cavaliers with recklessly ready swords and a passion for night-road romance. Ever the moon rides high over Paris, and horses gallop swiftly through the night. King's business or the business of a lady; rescue, sortie or assault, it is all one to the brawling, gallant, turbulent, tender gentlemen at arms. And, inevitably, they are the best swordsmen of their day.

It is *not* too bad that hundreds of such romances find publishers and readers, even when they are of infinitely less merit than those of Stephens and Stanley Weyman, his English counterpart. Tastes are as catholic as bookshelves are wide, and the most discriminating reader may admit the excellence of the Russians without yielding an ounce of his liking for the Romantics. Perhaps, after all, it is only a matter of alphabetic arrangement; and after Dostoievsky, on the shelves, come Doyle and Dumas. It is well to bear in mind Mr. Cabell's statement, already quoted, which, argued to a relentless conclusion, comes to this: that first class art not only seldom reproduces its surroundings, but seldom deals with recognizable realities—at least, with those homespun minutiae that ordinarily, in our sophistication, we regard as realities.

Robert Neilson Stephens wrote other books, of varying interest and merit, and "A Continental Dragoon" had a fair success on the stage under the title of "Miss Elizabeth's Prisoner." Neither the book nor the play, it must be admitted, was particularly good. He was not much

happier in "Philip Winwood;" and in "The
Mystery of Murray Davenport," he proved the
inability of a man saturated with the past to write
a novel about the present—even a light story
calculated only to sell. In none of his historical
tales, however, did he fail to capture in some
degree that glamor of other days. His setting
invariably was colorful, and one book, at least,
"Captain Ravenshaw," of its kind was excellent.
It is enough perhaps to write one good book, if
only people will remember and read it.

The charm that many readers found in Stephens' work, was the charm that his friends found
in Stephens. His personality was vivid. His
bookishness drew him to many; he was a profound student of past periods. All admired his
courage, for he fought an heroic battle with
disease until the end, and died tragically before
forty.

He had an odd trick of embroiling himself
with his characters. Although conscientiously
careful in his choice of names for the men and
women with whom he peopled his books, he was
forever corresponding, it seemed, with the surviving members of some ancient House, whose
title unwittingly he had appropriated. Usually,
he extricated himself from these humorous difficulties with one delightful letter to the indignant

inquirers; sometimes it took two or three. He
established a very pleasant relation, at one time,
with the then existing heads of the old Welsh
family of Phillipps, after first exciting their surprise by his use of their patronymic, and his
knowledge of their traditions, in "A Continental
Dragoon."

When he was casting about for descriptive
paraphernalia in connection with the tale which
later became "Philip Winwood," he visited a
public gallery in London, in which city he happened to be at the time. Being particularly
taken by a handsome old fellow, done in oil by
some early English painter, he stopped before
the portrait and learned that the subject of his
admiration once had been Sir Ralph Winwood.
This struck him as being a fine-sounding name
indeed, and he announced his intention to use it.
As the hero of his unwritten story reminded him
of Sir Philip Sidney, he substituted Philip for
Ralph, and thought he had done a good day's
work. On at least two other occasions, however,
he had been obliged to explain to relatives, and
he confessed to his wife that he felt some mis-
givings.

These were promptly justified on the appearance of the book. He received a letter from a
Sir Ralph Winwood, existing holder of the title.

This time the communication was unusually amiable, to his pleased surprise, and another pleasant relationship was established. Stephens, congratulating himself on the happy thought that had led him to exchange Ralph for Philip, wondered if his luck had turned and, for a time, it seemed that it had. Then he published "Captain Ravenshaw."

This name, Stephens had dug out of an old book; and he had exercised considerable ingenuity in an effort to locate a surviving Ravenshaw before adopting it. It was a ravishing name, and the author was properly gratified to discover that the family that had owned it was no longer existent. His publisher, L. C. Page of Boston, also liked the sonorous syllables, and made certain secret inquiries and researches on his own account, at the end of which he unearthed the ancient coat of arms of the "extinct" family, and emblazoned it magnificently on the cover of the book. It was a stunning affair.

Then Stephens, on a day, opened his morning mail and pulled a long face over a lengthy and irate epistle from India. The signature was that of a Colonel Ravenshaw, an elderly military gentleman. The Colonel stormed through several inky sheets, and it developed that, while the story was "not half bad," he objected seriously to his name being given a man who was a "damned villain and a depraved knave." Also, he wished to know by what right his coat of arms was flaunted on the cover of the volume.

A number of letters was exchanged, and the Colonel perceptibly thawed. In the end, he melted completely; and some time later he hobnobbed with the author in London.

Gossip of Robert Neilson Stephens is pleasant, for he was the sort of man whose memory lends itself to whimsical reminiscence. He was not conspicuously "uppish," although he made no secret of his liking for the English nobility, and he had many friends who wore resounding titles. This did not prevent of his joking quietly at their expense, when occasion offered, and one of his remarks about the King of England—Edward VII—is still recalled.

When "Miss Elizabeth's Prisoner" was playing in London, King Edward and Queen Alexandra attended a performance, and, liking the drama, insisted on congratulating the author. With this precedent, the nobility flocked to the theatre the evening after the red-letter occurence, and Stephens was congratulated by the Duke and Duchess of Fife and the Princess Victoria. The author, unabashed, shook the hands of his distinguished guests, and smilingly remarked to

the others about him, "Sweet of the King, isn't
it? He comes himself, likes my play, and next
night sends the children!"

Robert Neilson Stephens is dead, and I am
afraid his books are by way of becoming forgotten. Perhaps it was inevitable that this should
be so, but it is too bad. He was an honest and
skilful entertainer, and less worthy books than
his are praised, and praised unduly. I hope that
I may be the means of calling to someone's admiring attention, if nothing more, that good
Shakespearian chronicle called "Captain Ravenshaw." It deserves its two inches of shelf room
in anybody's bookcase, beside that other admirable presentation of Elizabethan manners, Mr.
John Bennett's "Master Skylark," which still,
I believe, is known to and appreciated by wise
children.

Y. E. A. AND A BOTTLE OF RUM

LIVING to-day in Louisville, Kentucky, is an elderly gentleman, with a white mustache and a droll eye, slightly deaf and soft-spoken, who some day will be just such a subject for gossip as are Goldsmith, Charles Lamb and Eugene Field. Not perhaps for the masses; but certainly for the members of that inner circle who appreciate the finer flowerings of letters, the permanent contribution rather than the ephemeral success. I can not better introduce him than by re-telling the story of a famous controversy.

In the early fall of the year 1914, a considerable dispute arose concerning the authorship of a poem. In the *mêlée* of words, Walt Mason justified his existence, Champion I. Hitchcock produced an unique volume, and the New York Times made a gaudy spectacle of itself. The poem was that delightful piece of rhythmic devilry which will instantly be recalled by its opening lines:

> Fifteen men on the dead man's chest,
> Yo-ho-ho and a bottle of rum!

A correspondent wrote to the *Times,* requesting the poem; another correspondent furnished

it, shockingly mutilated, claiming to have found
it written on the fly-leaf of a book dated 1843.
The *Times* spoke sapiently about this "rough, unstudied sailor's jingle." Immediately the fight
was on. Walt Mason vigorously rebuked the
newspaper for its characterization, and furnished
the name of the poem's author—Young E. Allison. The venerable *Times* dissented, thinking it
"unlikely that Mr. Allison wrote the famous old
chanty," and finally Champ Hitchcock wrote a
monograph to prove it, and published it himself,
achieving at once a triumph of truth and of book-
making. The *Times* gracefully recanted, and
again all was well.

Thus did one of the world's most famous fugitive poems receive, at length, the full publicity
it deserved. Since that time, a host of admirers
have paid this masterpiece the tribute of un-
qualified admiration, and not long before his
death James Whitcomb Riley added a stanza, in
jest, which is practically unknown. It ran:

> Fifteen men on the dead man's chest,
>   Yo-ho-ho and a bottle of rum!
> Young E. Allison done all the rest,
>   Yo-ho-ho and a bottle of rum!
> He's sung this song for you and me,
> Jest as it wuz—or ort to be—
> Clean through time and eternity,
>   Yo-ho-ho and a bottle of rum!

Before that, Riley had called the poem "delish-amous," and "a masterly and exquisite ballad of delicious horrificness." But Riley missed an opportunity; in my opinion, the last line of his stanza should have been written, "Y. E. A. and a bottle of rum!"

What Riley meant by his stanza was that Allison took the original four lines, as they occur in Stevenson's "Treasure Island," and wrote the tremendous poem known as "Derelict," using the Stevenson quatrain as a text; and that is the truth. Like other readers, Allison was captured by the grisly charm of the chorus, and wondered where Stevenson had got it, and whether there were any more of it. Like one or two others, he determined to finish it himself. Allison, I think, never was certain whether the original stanza was Stevenson's own composition; but recently I became curious on this score, and now I am enabled to quote from a letter written by Mr. Lloyd Osbourne, stepson of R. L. S., for whom "Treasure Island" was written and to whom the work was dedicated. Says Mr. Osbourne: " 'Fifteen Men' was wholly original with Stevenson, and it has always been a regret to me that he never saw the Allison extension of the chanty."

But long before the *Times* controversy brought the whole matter before the public, an apprecia-

tive circle knew the name of "Derelict's" author,
and cherished the poem. As first written, it contained three stanzas, and was entitled "A Piratical Ballad." It was set to music by Henry Waller, published by William A. Pond & Co., and
sung by Eugene Cowles; this was in 1891. But
the trio of ragged stanzas, as he called them, did
not satisfy Allison, and during the next four or
five years he amended and changed and added
and polished until the result was the poem as it
is known to-day. First publication of the whole
work was in the Louisville *Courier-Journal;* re-
printings have not yet ceased, nor are they likely
to. At just what point an exchange-editor's
scissors slipped is not known, but for a number
of years the reprinted ballad was attributed to
that prolific writer, "Anonymous;" then followed
the *Times* episode and Champ Hitchcock's book
reproducing the original scraps of manuscripts.

Few poems have received such careful, persistent revision; one thinks of Poe's explanation of
the development of "The Raven," in "The Philosophy of Composition." Allison is not yet *quite*
satisfied with his achievement; he believes there
should be one more stanza in which Captain
Flint's green parrot should be celebrated, with
that immortal squawk—"Pieces of eight!" Be
this as it may, from first to last there have been

word-, line-, and punctuation-changes of the
shrewdest sort, until at present the nuances are as
perfect as the author can make them. From the
beginning, Allison's intention has been to complete the poem as Stevenson himself might have
done, and explanation of the italicized fifth stanza is found in that intention; it is a delicate inti-
mation that the theme of a woman is foreign to
the main idea.

The following version of the ballad incorpo-
rates its author's final revisions:

DERELICT

A Reminiscence of Treasure Island.

Fifteen men on the dead man's chest—
Yo-ho-ho and a bottle of rum!
Drink and the devil had done for the rest—
Yo-ho-ho and a bottle of rum!
(Cap'n Billy Bones his song)

Fifteen men on the dead man's chest—
Yo-ho-ho and a bottle of rum!
Drink and the devil had done for the rest—
Yo-ho-ho and a bottle of rum!
The mate was fixed by the bos'n's pike,
The bos'n brained with a marlinspike,
And Cookey's throat was marked belike
It had been gripped
By fingers ten;
And there they lay,
All good dead men,

Like break-o'-day in a boozing ken—
    Yo-ho-ho and a bottle of rum!

Fifteen men of a whole ship's list—
    Yo-ho-ho and a bottle of rum!
Dead and bedamned, and the rest gone whist—
    Yo-ho-ho and a bottle of rum!
The skipper lay with his nob in gore
Where the scullion's axe his cheek had shore—
And the scullion he was stabbed times four.
        And there they lay,
            And the soggy skies
           Dripped all day long
             In up-staring eyes—
At murk sunset and at foul sunrise—
    Yo-ho-ho and a bottle of rum!

Fifteen men of 'em stiff and stark—
    Yo-ho-ho and a bottle of rum!
Ten of the crew had the murder mark—
    Yo-ho-ho and a bottle of rum!
'Twas a cutlass swipe, or an ounce of lead,
Or a yawing hole in a battered head,
And the scuppers glut with a rotting red.
        And there they lay—
           Aye, damn my eyes!—
          All lookouts clapped
           On paradise—
All souls bound just contrariwise—
    Yo-ho-ho and a bottle of rum!

Fifteen men of 'em good and true—
    Yo-ho-ho and a bottle of rum!
Every man jack could ha' sailed with Old Pew—
    Yo-ho-ho and a bottle of rum!
There was chest on chest full of Spanish gold,
With a ton of plate in the middle hold,
And the cabins riot of stuff untold.

And they lay there
   That had took the plum,
With sightless glare
   And their lips struck dumb,
While we shared all by the rule of thumb—
   Yo-ho-ho and a bottle of rum!

More was seen through the sternlight screen—
   Yo-ho-ho and a bottle of rum!
Chartings ondoubt where a woman had been—
   Yo-ho-ho and a bottle of rum!
A flimsy shift on a bunker cot,
With a thin dirk slot through the bosom spot
And the lace stiff-dry in a purplish blot.
   Or was she wench. . .
     Or some shuddering maid . . *?*
   That dared the knife
   And that took the blade!
By God! She was stuff for a plucky jade—
   Yo-ho-ho and a bottle of rum!

Fifteen men on the dead man's chest—
   Yo-ho-ho and a bottle of rum!
Drink and the devil had done for the rest—
   Yo-ho-ho and a bottle of rum!
We wrapped 'em all in a mains'l tight,
With twice ten turns of the hawser's bight,
And we heaved 'em over and out of sight—
   With a yo-heave-ho!
   And a fare-you-well!
   And a sullen plunge
   In the sullen swell—
Ten fathoms deep on the road to hell—
   Yo-ho-ho and a bottle of rum!

The first, second, third and last stanzas are
the best; the fourth and fifth, in my judgment,

are unnecessary and weaken the poem. In an earlier version, the third line of the second stanza was, "All of 'em down from the devil's own fist;" but the amended fancy is much happier. Comparison of the several versions printed since the poem's first appearance will show many changes, and in Allison's opinion, at least, there was good reason for every change.

In my search for Stevensoniana, and latterly for Allisoniana, I have unearthed two other "extensions" of "Fifteen Men," neither of the slightest literary importance, but both of considerable bibliographical importance. In the Chicago *Times-Herald,* many years ago, appeared an entertaining hoax, captioned "Stevenson's Sailor Song." Nobody signed it, but it was probably the work of some lesser contemporary of Eugene Field. The anonymous newspaper writer, after recalling Stevenson's refrain in "Treasure Island," alleges to have come upon a group of "old-time sailors" on the Chicago river-front (!), lustily singing at their work on one of the big lake boats; they were "tugging at a hawser." A solo voice carried the main thread of the narrative, the other voices coming in on the refrain; and "here was Louis Stevenson's famous pirate song sung on a peaceful lake liner, with nothing more piratical in sight than the low, long, rakish trolley of an electric car on Clark Street!" Of course, the listener crept closer, and this is what he heard:

> Fifteen men on the dead man's chest,
>   Yo-ho-ho, and a bottle of rum!
> Drink and the devil had done for the rest,
>   Yo-ho-ho, and a bottle of rum!
>
> For they drank and drank and got so drunk,
>   Yo-ho-ho, and a bottle of rum!
> Each from the dead man bit a chunk,
>   Yo-ho-ho, and a bottle of rum!
>
> The bottle burst and the men accurst,
>   Yo-ho-ho, and a bottle of rum!
> Sucked his blood to quench their thirst,
>   Yo-ho-ho, and a bottle of rum!
>
> They sucked his blood and crunched his bones,
>   Yo-ho-ho, and a bottle of rum!
> When suddenly up came Davy Jones,
>   Yo-ho-ho, and a bottle of rum!
>
> 'My men,' says he, 'you must come with me,'
>   Yo-ho-ho, and a bottle of rum!
> And he grinned with a horrible kind of glee,
>   Yo-ho-ho, and a bottle of rum!
>
> Davy Jones had a big black key,
>   Yo-ho-ho, and a bottle of rum!
> It was for his locker beneath the sea,
>   Yo-ho-ho, and a bottle of rum!
>
> He winked and he blinked like an owl in a tree,
>   Yo-ho-ho, and a bottle of rum!
> And he sank them all to the bottom of the sea,
>   Yo-ho-ho, and a bottle of rum!

> Now, all take warning from this 'ere song,
>   Yo-ho-ho, and a bottle of rum!
> Never drink whisky so divilish strong,
>   Yo-ho-ho, and a bottle of rum!

The narrator concludes: "The song ended on an ear-piercing shriek, tremendous emphasis on the next to the last line. When inquiry was made of the sailors as to where they learned the song, they stared solemnly at the questioner until one black-haired giant, in a red woollen shirt, hitched his trousers defiantly and answered: 'We never learned it nowhere, we allers knowed it!' ".

That is obviously a hoax, with no particular intention to deceive, and it is also good fun. The stanzas are exceedingly clever regarded as a "rough, unstudied sailor's jingle," and the fellow who composed them knew what he was about. Allison's chanty is far too good to have been written by any but a very superior sort of sailor; but this newspaper-chanty might actually have been the work of a singing seaman. It is quite possible that the author of the newspaper article did not himself compose the chanty he quoted, that he heard it sung, someplace, and adopted and adapted it; but, granting that possibility, the suggestion that the chanty is an ancient one from which Stevenson drew his lines is only conceivable on the hypothesis that Lloyd Osbourne is in er-

ror (which is unlikely), and that Stevenson himself hinted an untruth. For, in a letter to Henley, dated August 25, 1881, R. L. S. makes the
following statement about "The Sea Cook" (later called "Treasure Island"), which was then
being written:

"It's all about . . . a sea song with a chorus, 'Yo-ho-ho and a Bottle of Rum,' (at the
third 'ho' you heave at the capstan bars,) which
is a real buccaneer's song, *only known to the crew
of the late Capt. Flint,* who died of rum at Key
West much regretted."

The italics, of course, are mine. In other
words, then, the song was known only to the fictitious crew of a fictitious captain; the extraordinary puppets of an invincible invalid who invented and wrote about pirates because it was neither
expedient nor possible to be one himself. In a letter to Colvin, in July, 1884, the invalid added:
" 'Treasure Island' came out of Kingsley's 'At
Last,' where I got 'The Dead Man's Chest.' "
That is, Stevenson had been reading Kingsley's
intolerably dull account of a visit to the West In-
dies, once a scene of splendid pirate activity, and
had run onto that single phrase, "the Dead Man's
Chest," descriptive, I believe, of a dangerous reef.
That would be enough for Stevenson, to whom

names and localities cried out for stories to be written around them.

Some years after the Chicago hoax, this same chanty, introducing Davy Jones, got itself into print as "Billy Bones's Fancy," with slight verbal changes and the injunction to sing it to the tune of "Blow the Man Down." It may be noted that in these versions the author takes the "dead man's chest" rather literally, and obviously himself sees a fantastic picture of fifteen men actually enthroned on the *breast* of a deceased pirate; or perhaps he is thinking of a sea chest conveniently beside the body. The better-informed Mr. Allison understood the reference, and was not misled by the "chest."

Then in 1902 there appeared "The Pirate Song," with music by Henry F. Gilbert, and "words adapted from Stevenson's 'Treasure Island.' Additional stanzas by Alice C. Hyde." This is an admirable musical *macabre,* although it is not as good as Waller's. The verses by Miss Hyde are ordinary. To complete the note, however, they are here transcribed:

> Fifteen men on a dead man's chest,
>   Yo! ho! ho! and a bottle of rum!
> Drink and the devil had done for the rest,
>   Yo! ho! ho! and a bottle of rum!

Hate lies close to love of gold,
      Yo! ho! ho! and a bottle of rum!
Dead men's secrets are tardily told,
      Yo! ho! ho! and a bottle of rum!

Dead men only the secret shall keep,
      Yo! ho! ho! and a bottle of rum!
So bare the knife and plunge it deep,
      Yo! ho! ho! and a bottle of rum!

Fifteen men on a dead man's chest,
      Yo! ho! ho! and a bottle of rum!
Drink and the devil had done for the rest,
      Yo! ho! ho! and a bottle of rum!

Possibly there are other versions builded upon the original quatrain, but I have not seen them. A good musical setting of Allison's version was published for male voices, in 1907, by the Boston Music Company. Francis Campbell is the composer, and the piece is called "On Board the Derelict."

To come back to Allison: I suppose there is little doubt that his fame is assured by this remarkable poem, so far as it is possible to predict the vagaries of fame's erratic flight; and it is pleasant to know that the controversy over authorship was happily adjusted in his lifetime. Without Champ Hitchcock and the other champions, the dispute might have been continued indefinitely, for Allison himself is far too retiring an individual to push his own claims beyond a modest statement of fact. It is his notion that "these things take care of themselves, and usually work out all right." I am cynical enough to doubt it.

Now when a reader ecstatically has "discovered" this famous ballad, and has learned it by heart, and has run around chanting it to his friends, his first thought is likely to be: "What else has this Allison man done?" And he will hasten off to book-shops and libraries intent on procuring a whole volume of equally delectable and fascinating pirate songs. I made this heartbreaking search years ago; but it was a long time before I found a trace of Young E. Allison. Then I met a man who knew him. Then I met Allison himself. I wish it were permitted me to eulogize at length this delightful man, but here is not the place.

Young E. Allison is the editor of the Insurance Field, with headquarters in Louisville. That has been his profession and his home for a great many years. All day long his head is filled with figures, as for many years was Lamb's. In odd moments, when he happens to feel like it, he writes verses and essays; less often he writes short stories. At long intervals he is dragged from his home and cozened into making addresses, but the occasion must be a rare one—the

birthday anniversary of Burns accomplished it
once. His remarks at the memorial service for
his friend Riley were perfect and memorable.

I think he does not regret the little time left
by his duties for literature; he is an excellent
economist and while his collected works will be
few, they will be precious. No other poem by
him compares with "Derelict;" the rest are engaging but, I think, ephemeral. Years ago, he
wrote a newspaper novel, "The Passing of Major
Kilgore," a good story; but it is buried in the
files of a defunct magazine. His short stories
and his essays also for the most part are hidden
in old files. The librettos of two comic operas by
him, one of them a collaboration, once were
printed; but they are now almost unprocurable.

What else, then, is there that may bring happiness to the admirer of "Derelict," on his Twistian search?

There is "The Delicious Vice," if one can
come across it. The editions (there have been
two) were limited, and both are out of print.
Since the death of Charles Lamb, who now hob-
nobs genially, it is to be hoped, with Walter Savage Landor, in some paradisal inn, no more delightfully bookish volume has come from any
press. "The Delicious Vice," to which Allison
pleads guilty, is novel-reading. The sub-title

of the slim volume is, "Pipe Dreams and Fond
Adventures of an Habitual Novel-Reader among
Some Great Books and their People." It is the
friendliest book imaginable; in it, a confirmed
bookman takes you by the hand and leads you
through his library—and there is not a Guten-
berg Bible in the collection! Not a Caxton, not
an Elzevir, not a Kelmscott. Instead, you meet
(*again,* it is assumed) "Robinson Crusoe," and
"The Three Musketeers," very little of Dickens
and Scott, every line of Stevenson, and every
juvenile of importance from Beadle's Dime Library to "Kingston and Ballantyne the brave."
Through the book, a glittering thread, runs Allison's quaint humour, Allison's high spirits, Allison's remarkable personality.

Young E. Allison has done many fine things,
and some day they will be diligently sought out
and reprinted; but if he had done nothing else
he would still stand high in the affection of discriminating readers because of "Derelict" and
"The Delicious Vice."

"BLACK BEAUTY" AND ITS AUTHOR

CENTENARY celebrations are posterity's tributes to the favored children of fame; sometimes they are tardy acknowledgments to genius. Too often does genius sup late, and sometimes it does not sup at all. One wonders whether, on the thirtieth day of March, 1920, in all the world there was a single thought of Anna Sewell. Certainly no celebration marked the day. Despite the unique popularity of her single book, there seems never to have been much interest in Miss Sewell as a person. Yet it has been asserted that since the invention of printing, than *Black Beauty* only the Bible has found a wider distribution; and it is certain that more than any other single agency this humane classic has improved the lot of the captive horse. The book has lived; the author has been forgotten.

Anna Sewell died in pain within a year of the success of her first and only volume. The story of her life explains the deep humanity of *Black Beauty*. Few lives perhaps have been less eventful in their worldly aspects than that of the crippled Quaker girl; yet it was a life freighted with great emotional crises, spiritual distresses, and physical pain. She was born at Yarmouth,

in England, on March 30, 1820, the first child
of Isaac and Mary (Wright) Sewell; she died
on April 25, 1878, at Old Catton, near Norwich.
So much one may find in certain biographical
dictionaries, but for the most part there has been
nothing whatever said about the author of a book
millions of copies of which have been printed in
a dozen languages.

She was born in a troublous moment for her
parents. Her father's business—a partnership—
was in danger, and within a few days of his
daughter's birth Isaac Sewell was looking for
another place. Almost simultaneously, her
mother's father suffered reverses that lost him
all his property, so that there could be no assistance from that quarter, while an unhappy chance
that led Isaac Sewell to attempt shop-keeping in
London immediately proved disastrous. Another partnership was equally unfortunate, and was
soon dissolved, leaving Isaac Sewell penniless;
and in this black hour was born Anna's brother,
Philip. Mrs. Sewell was ordered by a physician
to leave London, the furniture was sold to pay
the family's debts, and after an agony of weeks
the Sewells, aided by friends, located in a small
house at Dalston, where in straitened circumstances they lived for the next nine or ten years,

and where the children's morning years were
spent.

It was a happy enough childhood, all in all, for
Mrs. Sewell was a remarkable mother, and Isaac
Sewell was a kind, if unfortunate father. But
strict economy had to be practiced at Dalston, and
to earn money for the purchase of books wherewith to educate her children, Mrs. Sewell herself
wrote a book—*Walks with Mamma*—the first of
a long line of juveniles chiefly in words of one syl-
lable. The required educational volumes were
purchased and the studies went forward, aided by
little local journeys through which the children added to their knowledge of natural history, a subject in which they delighted. Occasionally they
visited the British Museum, and once on a visit to
Folkestone they met Gerard Edward Smith, a
noted botanist, who manifested interest in the children and proved it by kindly instruction. Ento-
mology fascinated both mother and daughter, but
they never compassed death to make a collection—
after one tearful trial. They painted the captured moths and butterflies while they lay under
glass, and for the rest depended upon their quick
eyes and wits.

An early instance of Anna's efforts in behalf
of brute humanity (although in this case it was
bird humanity) is related by her mother. A

"sportsman" of the neighborhood had shot a blackbird, which fell into the front garden of the Sewell place. The man came to the gate to take possession of his prize. Anna rushed to the door. With an obsequious smile the man said: "If you please, Miss, will you let me take my bird?" "No!" cried the child passionately. "Thee cruel man, thee shan't have it, at all!" And the man did not have it.

To this period belong certain faded old papers from which pertinent extracts may be made. They are Mrs. Sewell's comments on her children. One paper is headed, "Anna Sewell's Birthday," and reads in part:

"Anna Sewell has this day completed her ninth year, and is in many respects a delight and comfort to her mother, who, that she may be able to test her progress from year to year, wishes now to write a short account of her attainments in learning, and of the qualities of her mind." Follows entire approbation of Anna's truth and candor, and of her progress in some of her studies; then: "Much disposed to idle over lessons and work. She needs to get the habit of a cheerful surrender of her own will—to give up entirely telling tales of her brother. She begins to be useful to her mother, but is not tidy. In

everything her mother hopes she will be improved
by another year."

It was a high standard of perfection that Mrs.
Sewell set for her children, and it is likely that no
such paragons of virtue ever existed as the mother's dream of her perfected offspring; but these
were early Victorian days, and this was a Quaker
mother. If the young Sewells fell short of their
mother's highest desire, they came nearer than
most children, it would appear, to that unique
perfection dreamed of by such mothers as Mary
Sewell. Anna and Philip probably were older
than their years, but they were not prigs.

Whilst living at Dalston, Anna dislocated her
elbow, which was some time in recovering its
strength; speaking to her aunt of this painful
incident the small sufferer said: "I bored it well!"
So she might have spoken of the painful circumstances of her later life, for she had a cheerful,
patient courage. But more troubled waters were
ahead. The family removed to a larger place
in the neighborhood, calling it Palatine Cottage,
and undertook to increase its small income by
keeping cows and selling the milk; but a laborer
and his wife who had been engaged to look after
the stock decamped with a large sum of money
gathered from the country clientele, leaving the
Sewells again in dreary circumstances. On the

heels of this blow came the worst that was to fall.

Anna now was going to school and, returning home one day, was overtaken by a heavy fall of rain. Having no umbrella, she started to run. The carriage road sloped steeply downward to the garden gate, and just as the small runner reached the gate she fell. A badly sprained ankle was the immediate result; later a life of frustration and renunciation. Hearing her cry out, her mother hastened to her assistance and helped her indoors, little thinking that the bright and active girl thenceforward was to be a cripple; but Anna Sewell never again walked upright like other girls.

Mistakes were made; in those days doctors were less wise than to-day. As far as the family's circumstances would permit, everything was tried; and some of the treatments seriously aggravated the girl's trouble. She never was cured. Years of life were ahead of her, no one of which was entirely to be free of pain. After her death, her mother wrote: "All who knew her loved her. . . Her sufferings never made a gloom or a cloud in the house. . . She was my sunshine always; there never came the slightest cloud between us. Thank God!"

Thus, after her accident, did Anna Sewell

reach that high standard of perfection that was her mother's dream.

The year that followed Anna's accident was an eventful one for the Sewells. Palatine Cottage was rented, Mrs. Sewell left the Society of Friends, and Isaac Sewell determined to accept a position with a bank that was to be opened in Brighton. Removal to Brighton in 1836 brought new interests, and for a little time Anna's walking powers seemed to increase. With her mother she carried on a work begun at Dalston to relieve the sufferings of the poor, and the pair accomplished some notable good in the Brighton workhouse. In large measure, too, Mrs. Sewell's unsettled religious views had found sanctuary in the Church of England, and both children were communicants of that church. The family left Brighton in 1845 and went to reside in Lancing, some ten miles distant, but Isaac Sewell continued to go to Brighton daily, so that a pony chaise became part of the household equipment; and in driving her father to and from Shoreham station, Anna was unconsciously laying away material for *Black Beauty*.

Anna Sewell, with her mother, her brother, and her mother's sister, visited Germany in 1846, but of this visit there is left little record. In 1849 another removal was made, this time to

Hayward's Heath, and in the same year Philip, an engineer, married. The following year he undertook important work in Spain, and went to live in that country. The others sustained a further removal in 1853, going to Grayling Wells, near Chichester. Most of these years seem to have been largely occupied by a weary search after improvement in Anna's health, and in 1856 mother and daughter went to Marienberg, where Anna was left for nearly a year, returning in better health than she had known since her accident. She was able to walk a bit, and there was a memorable holiday at Dorking when mother and daughter knew their first little space of unclouded happiness in many years. All day long they walked or sat among spring flowers, reveling in the beauty of the place; and when at evening they returned to their lodging they were so interested in Carlyle's *Past and Present* that only with difficulty could they persuade themselves to go to bed; so they drank coffee to keep off sleep and lengthen each happy day. A quarter of a century afterward Mrs. Sewell spoke of that book with enthusiasm.

All this time Mrs. Sewell had been writing, and a number of little books had come from the press with her name upon the title-pages. Anna was her mother's chief and best critic. "If I

can pass my Nannie," Mrs. Sewell used to say,
"I don't fear the world after that."

In the fall of the year 1857, the Sewells visited
Philip and his family at Santander, in Spain,
and a new world of beauty was opened to mother
and daughter. Meanwhile, it had been decided
again to move, and upon their return the house
at Grayling Wells was given up, and Blue
Lodge, Wick, was chosen to be the next home.
The place was within driving distance of either
Bath or Bristol; it stood between the villages
of Siston and Wick, although it was a long way
from either, and the inconveniences of the place
made it anything but cheap. But in spite of
forebodings, the lonely spot proved the very
place for authorship, and here all the chief works
of Mrs. Sewell were composed. Visitation of the
poor commenced again, and an active temperance
work was carried on. In a letter written in December of 1858, the mother speaks of Anna as
being "quite lame, and her head very weak, but
according to her measure she is very active; and
her back being strong now she can ride alone on
the pony to the school often in the week."

A friend who stayed at Blue Lodge for three
days in the summer of 1863, tells of reading a
manuscript for Mrs. Sewell's criticism; the en-

terprise went forward in a tree-arched walk in
the grounds. The reminiscence continues:

"Meanwhile Anna would appear from time to
time at the garden door of the house, shading her
eyes with her hand, and trying to discover our
whereabouts, anxious to meet any possible want
or wish of her mother's. At that time a weakness
of the limbs confined her much indoors, except
for the almost daily drives with her mother to
the village, to visit their cottage friends and su-
perintend the workingmen's club they had established. These drives often fell on cold and
wet winter nights, and I remember Anna's gentle
triumph in having falsified her friends' predic-
tions of physical harm to herself from the ex-
posure, her mother gaily adding, 'In fact, we've
come to regard night drives in an open carriage
in bad weather as a positive cure for delicacy.'
At the time I speak of, Anna was unable to stand
for more than a few seconds at a time, though she
moved freely about the house. Wherever Mrs.
Sewell and I might be working at our proofs,
or discussing questions they suggested, if household affairs brought the daughter to her mother's side, she was obliged to kneel on the nearest
support for the minute she remained. But her
general appearance had little or nothing of the
invalid, and the calm radiance of her expressive

face was remarkable. My husband chancing once
to meet her in a shop in Bath, came home, saying,
'I've just seen Anna Sewell's beautiful face.'
And beautiful indeed it was, with the beauty of
nobility and purity."

The last winter at Blue Lodge was that of
1863. The life there, lively enough for the ladies, was dull for Isaac Sewell, and in 1864 some
occupation adapted to his declining years (He
was then seventy-one years of age) appears to
have offered in Bath. Removal followed, and
Moorlands, within a little walk of Bath, became
their home. A little later, in 1866, Philip came
to reside in Norwich, and not long afterward his
wife died, leaving him with seven children. Then
Isaac Sewell's occupation came to an end, and
once more the family removed, this time to its
native county, and settled at Old Catton, not far
from Philip's home at Clare House. It was
the last move; the little white house became the
home of seventeen years; the wanderings of the
Sewells were at an end.

The summer of 1870 appears to have been the
last time mother and daughter were able to be
out in the sunshine together. Toward the end of
that year the shadow of death began to steal over
the little white house, and never was wholly lifted
until the end. In November there are allusions

to attacks of faintness which the doctor thought might be a precursor of "something serious." This was the beginning of Anna's mortal illness, and for the next eight years she was her mother's constant care. When all hope had passed that Anna would be able to drive about again, the pony and cart were given up. Mr. Sewell became increasingly feeble. Meanwhile, Philip had married again, and his wife was of great assistance.

Considering the distressing nature of her malady, the entries in Anna's journal at this time show a surprising list of small events and hospitalities. Here are some tell-tale passages:

August 9 [1871]. Mrs. Riches' class of thirty girls came to tea.

Sept. 1. We gave a tea and frolic to thirty-four children, Miss H.'s Band of Hope. G. and F. helped.

Sept. 13. Mother's Sun Lane Infants (50) had tea and play. A. and A. helped famously.

Jan. 1, 1872. Mother went, with our children, to St. Faith's Union, and gave toys and presents.

Jan. 23. Jonathan Grubb came.

Jan. 26. I am quite poorly with pain.

This last—"quite poorly"—seems to have been the strongest expression of suffering that Anna permitted herself. The year closes with, "I am poorly."

Meanwhile, *Black Beauty* had been begun. The first mention of the story occurs in her journal under date of November 6, 1871: "I am writing the life of a horse, and getting dolls and boxes ready for Christmas." There is no further entry on the subject until December 6, 1876; then: "I am getting on with my little book, 'Black Beauty.'" The next is dated August 21, 1877, and reads: "My first proofs of 'Black Beauty' are come—very nice type."

There is an appealing modesty about this record; and it is a poignant thought that this "beautiful equine drama" was almost entirely thought out on the sofa where so much suffering daily was endured. When she was capable of supporting the fatigue of writing, the work was done with a pencil, and Mrs. Sewell, sitting beside her, received the paper from the tired hand and made a fair copy of it. One of the few existing fragments of Anna Sewell's manuscript bears upon her famous tale; it was written not long before her death. She wrote:

"I have for six years been confined to the house and to my sofa, and have from time to time, as I was able, been writing what I think will turn out a little book, its special aim being to induce kindness, sympathy, and an understanding treatment of horses. In thinking of Cab-horses, I have been led to think of Cabmen, and I am anxious, if I can, to present their true condition, and their great difficulties, in a correct and telling manner.

"Some weeks ago I had a conversation at my open window with an intelligent Cabman who was waiting at our door, which has deeply impressed me. He led the conversation to the Sunday question, after telling me that he never plied on the Sabbath. I found there was a sore, even a bitter feeling against the religious people who, by their use of cabs on Sunday, practically deny the Sabbath to the drivers. 'Even ministers do it, Ma'am,' he said, 'and I say it's a shame upon religion.' Then he told me of one of the London drivers who had driven a lady to church—as she stepped from the cab, she handed the driver a tract on the observance of the Sabbath. This naturally thoroughly disgusted the man. 'Now, Ma'am,' said my friend, 'I call that hypocrisy— don't you?' I suppose most of us agree with him, and yet it might not have been done hypocritically—so few Christians apparently realize the responsibility of taking a cab on Sunday."

What was the germ of *Black Beauty?* It appears to have been Horace Bushnell's *Essay*

on Animals, quoted to Anna by a friend, Mrs.
Bayly. This is Mrs. Bayly's account of the incident:

"It was in the summer of 1862 that I first met
Mrs. Sewell, at the home of her old friend Mrs.
Ellis, at Hoddesdon. In the following summer
I had the great pleasure of paying her a short
visit at Blue Lodge, Wick. She was then engaged in writing the last chapters of her book,
'Thy Poor Brother.' As we three sat together in
the drawing-room, she read me some of the earlier
chapters. They were so suggestive, we talked
and talked, complaining of nothing but the lapse
of time. Anna was lying on the sofa—her mother sitting at her feet, with one hand rubbing the
lame foot, with the other holding the manuscript
out of which she was reading.

"The parting came all too soon. In the after-
noon it poured with rain. When the carriage that
was to take me to the station came to the door,
Anna was standing in the hall, enveloped in a
large mackintosh. The future writer of 'Black
Beauty' was to be my driver. I found that she
and her mother were in the habit of driving out
on most days, without attendance, the understanding between themselves and their horse being perfect. The persistent rain obliged us to
keep up our umbrellas. Anna seemed simply to

hold the reins in her hand, trusting to her voice to give all needed directions to her horse. She evidently believed in a horse having a moral nature, if we may judge by her mode of remonstrance. 'Now thee shouldn't walk up this hill— don't thee see how it rains?' 'Now thee must go a little faster—thee would be sorry for us to be late at the station.'

"I think it was during this drive that I told Anna of something Horace Bushnell had written about animals. Soon after the publication of 'Black Beauty' I had a little note from her, written from her sofa, in which she says:

" 'The thoughts you gave me from Horace Bushnell years ago have followed me entirely through the writing of my book, and have, more than anything else, helped me to feel it was worth a great effort to *try,* at least, to bring the thoughts of men in harmony with the purposes of God on this subject.' "

During the year 1876, Anna was sometimes able to dictate passages of *Black Beauty,* and the story was completed late in 1877. Isaac Sewell continued to fail, and Mrs. Sewell herself, that iron woman, was liable to turns of severe but seldom disabling suffering, brought on by the constant strain. The book was published near the end of the year 1877, and Anna lived just long enough to hear of its remarkable success. Almost at once it rushed into a popularity undreamed-of by its author. The joy of the success of her book was almost too much for Anna's delicate frame, but the devoted mother rejoiced and collected the reviews of *Black Beauty* with a happiness greater than she had found in this phase of her own writing life. The work was virtually a gift to the world. The English publishers bought the book outright for a few pounds. And in America alone, in one edition or another, it has had a circulation to date of more than 3,000,000 copies!

An extraordinary fact is the lack of interest shown in the book by the Royal Society for the Prevention of Cruelty to Animals, for while it had an excellent general sale in England, it was not extensively used as propaganda until Mr. George T. Angell of Boston, founder of the Massachusetts Society for the Prevention of Cruelty to Animals, read it, recognized its missionary capabilities, and scattered it broadcast over the earth. After that of Anna Sewell herself, Mr. Angell's name must be that most closely associated with *Black Beauty*. In the history of humane literature the book holds a place unique; in the history of all literature it maintains its position as an authentic classic, not alone for children but for their parents. When the motion-picture drama was shown recently—a rather sad paraphrase of the book, for all its interest—the theaters were packed with men and women eager to see *Black Beauty* run upon the screen.

It is no small thing to have written *Black Beauty,* a book whose missionary achievements in its own field it is impossible to measure. It is unquestionably the most successful animal story ever written; and it would seem that its author should be something more than a name in the card-index of a library.

But of all her greater triumph Anna Sewell knew nothing. The first success was enough for her. Less than a year later she was dead. When the hearse that was to carry her to the burying-ground drew up at the door, Mrs. Sewell saw from the drawing-room window that the horses had bearing-reins. "Oh, this will never do!" she cried in distress, and hastened to order that the bearing-reins be removed from all the horses in the train. And so Anna's lifelong friend performed for her the last service she needed on earth, and no check-rein aggravated his proud spirit. Surely, never before nor since did horse draw so precious a freight.

Anna Sewell is buried in a quiet cemetery where her ancestors for many generations had been buried before her. It is in the village next to Buxton, and belongs to the Society of Friends, a sequestered spot surrounded by trees and a high hawthorne hedge, where the birds are never disturbed.

"HOME IS THE SAILOR—"

In Memoriam David Ker

D AVID KER is dead!
Who thrills at this cry? In whose heart
stirs a memory of that name? If there are living, within sound of my shout, men who were
boys in England or her colonies, perhaps in
America, twenty, thirty, forty years ago, surely
here is an announcement to touch their hearts and
bring back vanished days. The last of a great
quintette. For with the passing of David Ker
there passed the last, although for some the least,
of that notable galaxy of "boys' authors" that
made the last quarter of the nineteenth century
a golden age of juvenile literature. "Kingston
and Ballantyne the brave," as Stevenson called
them, went to their reward years ago; Henty and
Manville Fenn, who succeeded them, lived into
the early nineteen-hundreds and died within a
few years of each other; and now from the quiet
seclusion of a tiny English village, picturesquely
nestling in the heart of Surrey, comes word that
David Ker has joined his associates.

So quietly had the veteran author and ad-
venturer lived in his last years, and so few were
there to know and hear of his death, that, save

for an announcement in a small township journal published near his home, I believe this to be the first printed notice of his passing. Of the thousands of boys who in youth have loved him, I wonder how many, in manhood, have given him a thought. I should be sorry to think that in paying my own debt I am speaking only for myself.

This distinguished traveler and writer for boys died on August 9 last (1914), at his home, which upon an envelope is written, Tilden Cottage, Beacon Hill, Hindhead, Surrey, England. He was 71 years of age. His illness was of brief duration; his widow survives him. His immediate mourners, as enumerated in the local chronicle, were just four in number, including the widow; but these were all that mourned at the bier. I like to think that the boys of England, Australia and America will swell that brief muster to proportions that a grand duke might envy.

Singularly retiring in all matters pertaining to personal advertisement, Mr. Ker persistently deprecated suggestions of his friends and admirers that he write his reminiscences. No such volume has come from any press; so far as I have been able to ascertain only one notice of a biographical nature appeared in his lifetime. That was a short half-page in the Cosmopolitan Magazine, back in 1889. It is likely that Mr. Ker did not see it, that he never heard of it. He was leaving for Asia at the time, and the anonymous interviewer recorded a short conversation with the wanderer, concluding with an assertion to this effect: "If it were not that most of Mr. Ker's work is buried, unsigned, in the files of newspapers, he would be hailed as an explorer and traveler scarcely second to Stanley and Livingston." If David Ker himself had chosen to write his memories, what a book it would have been! His career was one of incredible adventure in the "uttermost parts of the earth."

David Ker was born at Bowden, near Birkenhead, England, in October, 1842. He came of an old Scottish family whose motto, *Sero, sed serio*—"Late, but in earnest!"—was given it by Robert Bruce, after the battle of Bannockburn, for which its members somewhat tardily had arrived. He was educated at Rugby and Oxford in the days when "Tom Brown" fought and prayed, and he became a fellow of Wadham College. Armed then with an excellent education, and driven by a roving spirit, he began a career of restless wandering possibly unparalleled by any traveler since the Wandering Jew. His extreme reticence makes difficult any immediate authentication of dates, but six of his early years

of manhood were spent in Russia, where he wrote
for the London *Morning Post* and the *Athe-
naeum* and became remarkably proficient in the
Russian language. And it is certain that the
early months of the year 1872 found him in
South America, for in May of that year he
climbed the famous Sugar-loaf Mountain, which
stands at the mouth of the harbor of Rio de Ja-
neiro, a fact to which he testifies in the preface
to his story, "The Wild Horseman of the Pam-
pas" (1875,) in which exciting narrative the then
unparalleled feat is performed by his boy hero.
Then, in 1873, he became correspondent of the
London *Daily Telegraph* in Central Asia, as-
signed to report the famous Khivan Expedition
which brought fame and, indirectly, death to the
American correspondent MacGahan. Disguised
as a Russian, he was the only Englishman who
succeeded in accompanying the Russian column.
Subsequently, he was discovered and barely escaped with his life. From this Bokharan experience dates his voluntary exile of many years,
and I think I do his memory no disservice in re-
peating the story; indeed it is frankly told by
Mr. Ker himself in the introduction to his story
of the campaign, "On the Road to Khiva"
(1874), a scarce volume for which I searched for
ten years. The situation perhaps is best revealed
in his own words:

The nature of the present work compels me to preface it with a few words about myself; but they shall be as few as possible. I make no apology for the delay which absence from home and severe illness have entailed upon me, knowing as I do that no man who has been condemned unheard can ever appeal in vain to the justice and good sense of an English public. So far as I can learn, the charges against me are as follows: 1. Having concocted letters at a distance from the scene of action; 2. Having wilfully sent false news of the fall of Khiva; 3. Having written magazine articles subsequent to my engagement with the *Daily Telegraph,* in direct violation of my own written contract; 4. Having filled my letters with extracts from my former articles.

To the first of these charges I reply, that the official passes given me to Orenburg, Fort No. 1, and Tashkent, General Kolpakovski's telegram to me at the latter place, with permission to visit Samarcand, and the letters written me *en route* by various Russian officers, are open to inspection. With regard to my "false telegram," I merely shared the general error produced by a garbled version of an actual event; and I sent the despatch only after receiving the same news from four officers in succession, whom I had every reason to believe well-informed. The articles alleged to have been written after my engagement with the *Daily Telegraph* were all written before it, that entitled, "From Sevastopol to Balaklava" being as old as February 5, 1873; but I readily admit sending home *en route* two unused papers which I had overlooked in the hurry of departure.

As to my self-repetition, I have no desire to excuse what is wholly inexcusable, but I should wish to say a few words on the subject nevertheless. What I had to do during my whole residence in the East was to sustain a very difficult assumed character, or rather series of characters, to obtain every kind of assistance and information from perfect strangers, without betraying my real object, to despatch letters and telegrams under the hourly risk of detection, and to force my way, with an English passport, into the heart of a region where the very presence of an Englishman is strictly prohibited. All this, superadded to growing ill-health, made the task of constant writing (when as yet there was little to write about) so intolerable, that I was glad to lessen the strain by using familiar words, even while conscious that I must have used them before. I had not, however, a single magazine with me; and I *did* see my "old savage" of the Crimea exactly reproduced, not merely on the Volga, but at least a dozen times in Turkestan.

With regard to the present work, it makes no pretence of being a history of the Khiva Expedition. I did my best to let at least one Englishman share the credit justly due to the brave man who represented America on that occasion; but, as events have fallen out, the honour is his, and his alone. But for the publication of my name, and my consequent seven weeks' imprisonment at Fort No. 1, I should have reached Khiva as I reached Samarcand; but although he has succeeded where I failed, I can none the less heartily wish him God-speed.

As for myself, I have as yet seen only one-half (the most important half, it is true) of Central Asia; and as soon as I have recovered [from] the effects of my last attempt (for it is no light thing to cross one thousand three hundred miles of desert under heavy rain, with a fever and three unhealed hurts) I shall try again. In the meantime, all that I wish to do is to tell my own story fairly, and to leave among my own countrymen, from whom I have been parted so many years, some better reputation than that of a liar and impostor.

This statement is dated January, 1874. The
honesty of it is so obvious that comment is unnecessary, save that in these newspaper days it
seems amazing that such an uproar should have
been created by the situation that gave the statement birth. For there was an uproar, and Mr.
Ker was unjustly and prematurely branded as
"liar and impostor." The *canard* hurt him, so
much so that, when he had proved the untruth
of the libel, he left England and came to live in
the United States.

Then, for some fourteen years, under a roving
commission from the New York *Times,* the ex-
patriate wandered up and down the world; and
the *Times* published his vivid correspondence
from every place under the sky. He visited India, Siam, Sumatra, Afghanistan, Ceylon, Bur-
mah, South Africa, West Africa. Off the coast
of West Africa, with his wife, he was shipwrecked. He traveled in Iceland, the Pharo Islands, Egypt, Baku (on the Caspian Sea), and
knew intimately every country in Europe and
the Americas. His headquarters throughout
these adventurous years was New York, and he
maintained a modest home in Brooklyn, where
one or two old friends still recall him with admiration and affection.

The indefatigable traveler published nineteen

books for boys almost entirely founded upon his own adventures and backgrounded by his extraordinary knowledge of history. He wrote hundreds of short stories and articles of travel, contributed dozens of serials (that never saw covers) to the *Boys' Own Paper* (London), and wrote more or less regularly for a series of magazines published by Messrs. Cassell, as well as for a number of American journals for the young. It is not to be supposed that he was much of a stylist, or that his tales belong to literature; but in vivid, galloping, adjectival narrative he had few equals. In my own boyhood, the youth of Canada worshipped him. Further, he was an astonishingly accomplished linguist, even for so ardent a traveler, and spoke fluently German, French, Russian and Portuguese, while he made shift to get along in Spanish and the other European languages, and possessed a fair acquaintance with such tongues as Malay and Hindustanee.

Mr. Ker had a remarkable memory. He could quote by the hour from the *Iliad* and *Odyssey,* in the original, and from the English classics; while two or three readings of a canto of Spenser were sufficient for him to remember the whole of what he had read. It is told of him that once, to a

blind man in France, he recited *Ivanhoe,* day after day, without a book, when the listener believed him to be reading the story.

So much I know, or have heard of Mr. Ker
through an all too brief correspondence with the
kindly old gentleman, and with certain of his
remaining friends; since his death, with his widow. Many times in my letters I asked him
to write the story of his life, or to allow others
to do it—even myself. Always his reply was
courteous but firm. Far from desiring his life-
story to be known, he explained in one letter, he
had himself destroyed everything upon which he
could lay hands which might aid a future biogra-
pher; even photographs were burned. The shadow of that miserable experience in London hung
over him to the last. Had that well-forgotten
editor been more charitable and less of a fool,
to-day the world might be richer by some magnificent volumes of travel and reminiscence.

Thus, my little memoir is likely to be all that
ever will find its way into print about a very
remarkable man. But should some devoted admirer, lacking my prohibitions and inhibitions,
ever care to attempt a biography, he will find
much to assist him in the numerous and often
voluminous footnotes in David Ker's tales for

boys. Such extraordinary footnotes they are!
I have read all of Mr. Ker's nineteen volumes
(my copy of "On the Road to Khiva" was Man
ville Fenn's, a presentation copy from the author), and as many of his magazine articles and
newspaper dispatches as I could procure; and in
each I have eagerly looked for footnotes. They
were always there; the thread-like record of his
life. The most incredible adventures described
are his own, and are authenticated by footnotes.
Lest his readers doubt the possibility of some
amazing feat of arms, some brilliant deed of der-
ring-do, chronicled in the adventures of a fictitious
boy-hero, Mr. Ker appends a footnote. The
note relates that this same adventure occurred to
Mr. Ker (sometimes with Mrs. Ker beside him,
for she accompanied him on many of his journeys) in some heathenish place the mention of
which sends one off to a geography, or conjures
nightmarish visions of brown-skinned natives,
swollen yellow streams, narrow mountain ledges,
and dense tropical jungles. I think if there is any
spot on the earth unvisited by this restless ad-
venturer, it has been discovered since his death.

In one book, I recall the astonishing episode of
a youth caught by a mountain train on a ledge of
rock so narrow that he might not stand aside to

allow the monster to pass. On one side a sheer
wall of rock, on the other a sheer drop of some
thousands of feet. Undismayed, our dauntless
youngster lies down upon his face in the exact
center of the track, between the rails—and the
train passes over him without touching his body.
The peculiar construction of the train, with which
our hero is familiar, makes this quite possible and
much less perilous than it looks. But it is, of
course, a moving recital, and Mr. Ker makes the
most of it. After a long breath, the ubiquitous
asterisk is noted; the reader dives for the footnote.   .   .

"Lest this be thought unworthy of belief, I
may say that the same thing happened to me on
a Brazilian mountain trail, and I managed to ex-
tricate myself from a ticklish position in the manner described.—D. K."

I am not certain that it was Brazil; but it
happened to Mr. Ker *somewhere*.

Again: our hero is in danger of being eaten
by sharks—not the same hero—and is desperately
swimming for life. The shark swiftly draws nearer. Afraid? No, the boy is not afraid; he finds
himself feeling surprised that he is not afraid,
and smiles as there begins to run in his head a
mad singsong learned years before at school. Of

course, he escapes the shark. Then the asterisk
and the footnote. . .

"I recall that, once in the Bay of (something),
when I was in danger from a shark, all that entered my head was an absurd speculation as to
whether I should enter the shark's mouth head-
first or broadside on!—D. K."

In "Unseen Depths," a tale of plantation life
in Ceylon, one of the young men of the narrative has a startling adventure with a wild ele-
phant. The angry beast, in the end, incautiously
steps to the edge of a precipice, the earth gives
way beneath his great weight, and down he
plunges into the gulf, leaving our hero safe
enough, but on the very brink of a new precipice
created by the mammoth's fall. The footnote
laconically recites that "most of the above inci-
dents are taken from an adventure of my own."
And in the same tale, a swarm of wild bees is
put to flight by torches made of dead boughs and
whirled through the thick of the living cloud, so
that hundreds of them are scorched up at a gesture. The footnote authenticates the fact, and
gives a clew to the date: "The same device enabled our party to beat off an attack of the terrible 'driver-ants' of West Africa, when Mrs.
Ker and I were wrecked there in July 1885.—
D. K."

From similar notes we learn that Mr. Ker climbed Adam's Peak, in Ceylon, in 1887; enjoyed a queer game on a vessel bound for Zululand; was passenger on board a vessel that was all but burned at sea; witnessed the eruption of the volcanic island of Krakatoa, in 1883; visited the ex-Ameer of Afghanistan in the Himalaya mountains; participated in the "shipwreck" of a Tartar wagon on a night journey through the Khanate of Khokand; camped with the Cossacks of the Don in 1869; had a landlord, in Hungary, called "Daniel Fish-bone;" was a fellow-passenger, in the Bay of Bengal, of the Maharajah of Vizianagram; took part in the Sikkim Expedition of 1888; was lost in the mountains of Tibet, and was on excellent terms with the medicine man of a tribe of Hottentots! Perhaps the exclamation point is not unjustified.

In effect, then, the life of David Ker *has* been written by himself; for, with a few exceptions, his books are books about himself. In most of them occurs a bronzed, bearded man of middle age, keen-eyed and resourceful, who is either a famous traveler, a noted author, or a war correspondent, and who is inevitably a great favorite with the youngsters about whom mainly the book is written. He tells them stories of wild adventure, sings them strange songs heard in remote and savage places, and is generally counselor, friend and leader. It is not straining, at all, to fancy this individual Mr. Ker himself. In two of the books—"Among the Dark Mountains" and "Swept Out to Sea"—this fascinating fellow is confessedly a writer of tales for boys, and in "Unseen Depths" he is called "Digby Knight," and turns a pun on the initials D. K. I think, therefore, we may assume that Mr. Ker conspicuously failed in his effort to destroy all material for a biography.

This is the man who died obscurely in a little village in Surrey, last August. It may be that his most faithful friends, the boys, thought of him as dead years ago, those who gave him thought as men. For some years he had not emerged from his seclusion, had written no books, and in the township he called home had taken no active part in public affairs. But he *told* stories, while he did not write them; the patients within the walls of a neighboring hospital, during the period of Mr. Ker's life at Hindhead, never will forget his visits and the hours he spent in *yarning* at their bedsides.

All I may now add to this slight chronicle is a paragraph from the first, heart-broken letter I had from Mrs. Ker, after his death:

"Mr. Ker and I were married in 1880. . .
He was a true poet, and had noble and lofty
ideals. He was loved and admired by his friends
and worshipped by his wife."

> *Under the wide and starry sky*
> *Dig the grave and let me lie.*
> *Glad did I live, and gladly die,*
> *And I laid me down with a will.*
> *This be the stone you grave for me:*
> *Here he lies where he longed to be.*
> *Home is the sailor, home from sea,*
> *And the hunter home from the hill.*

"GREAT HEART IS DEAD"

In Memoriam William Marion Reedy

OFTEN have I tried to speak my thoughts concerning Reedy living — in letters to Reedy, in talk with those that knew him not—and always with a sense of the futility of attempting to account for his charm; almost with a sense of frustration.

What can I say of Reedy dead?

A great man, a good man, a kindly man; simple, in the finest sense, and of an almost incredible honesty. Widely known and widely loved, he will be widely mourned. . . These are platitudes, poor enough tributes. They are the words and phrases commonly used when one dies who has been before the public—the stock phrases of the impromptu memorialist. But the commonplaces are the truths of life, and Death is the greatest platitude. And yet for Reedy there should be something finer, for he was unique.

I can no more pile up conventional adjectives for Reedy than Reedy could have piled up any kind for himself. Many will write of him; his measure of praise will be full. And some day the appraisal may be adequate and complete. Now, one's personal grief is all that may be set down, and one's profound belief that the world has lost one of its leading citizens.

In a world of hate and ignorance—and what is worse, educated ignorance—he was one of a small group that saw clearly and thought clearly. Yet his tolerance was admirable; his understanding and sympathy, rare. In a remarkable degree he was able to see with the other man's eyes, although in entire disagreement with the other man's conclusions. His common sense in economic matters was extraordinary, and it was that fundamental common sense and sanity that was his divining rod in distinguishing between the false and the true. His influence, in consequence, was salutary but kindly, and it must have been wide. And, like himself, the *Mirror* was unique, for Reedy was the *Mirror,* and the *Mirror* was Reedy. It will still be Reedy, if it lasts another hundred years.

That same common sense, backgrounded by enormous reading, made Reedy an excellent critic of letters. Publishers were proud to print his comments in their press notices, and on the jackets of their publications. But Reedy was a finer appreciator of literature than he was a critic—in the narrower sense of that word. His was a cathedral heart, and a catholic appreciation. Few men have so well bridged, in understanding, two periods of literature. Of the old school, in many ways, he was among the first to hail and defend the new school. In the columns of the *Mirror* first appeared Lee Masters' *Spoon River Anthology,* and such poets as Amy Lowell and Carl Sandburg were not infrequent contributors. Imagistes, "vers libertines" and the rest, found a ready champion in Reedy; loving the worthy old, he opened his arms to the worthy new. The authenticity of a writer's art and inspiration was all that concerned him as editor and critic. Not a few of the younger writers first came to prominence through Reedy; and his standards were high. While he aimed at timeliness, he was hospitable to anything that met the requirements of those careful standards, and the *Mirror* was one of too few journals of its kind in which timeliness was not an absolute requisite.

His own writing style was inimitable. It was schooner-rigged and rakish; a whimsical blend of the old and the new, of classical austerity and American journalese—sonorous, rollicking, often fantastic, always picturesque and decorative. Whatever his subject, he was always entertainingly readable; never by any chance dull. His "Reflections" were, I suppose, the most popular features of his journal, and their far range of interest was a thing to wonder at and admire.

Single-handed, he covered the world, and his comment was, for the most part, that of a wise and benevolent deity. . . Do you remember the closing lines of Lee Masters' fine poem to Reedy? So I see him.

Only once did I meet Reedy in the flesh, and then only for an hour or so in Masters' office in Chicago. He had run up to Chicago for something—I forget what—and I made my pilgrimage, and was made welcome. There was talk, chiefly from Reedy—fine, sonorous volumes of it, which one cannot help but call Johnsonian. He talked his "Reflections" with the charm and force of phrase, and with the rich pictorial suggestion, that made his written observations such delightful reading. It was a momentous meeting for me; how momentous I did not know until I heard of his death. But I had known Reedy long before that meeting, and I knew him for a little while after it. . . I shall look in vain, now, for the friendly, jovial letters I used to find in my mailbox; and there can be no others exactly like them. The good, kindly man! How distressed he was, upon a time, when he thought he had lost one of my unimportant manuscripts, and the trouble he was at, despite my protestations, to find it. He *did* find it, and then there was a letter. . .

"My dear Starrett: Please carefully uncurse me of all those curses you must have heaped upon my head; for lo, the lost is found. . ."

This is no time for anecdote, and indeed I have no anecdotes to tell—only a few words of gratitude (not tardy, I am happy to know) and affection, at the end of unforgettable association. I loved Reedy. I shall always love him.

> *And when he fell in whirlwind, he went down*
> *As when a lordly cedar, green with boughs,*
> *Goes down with a great shout upon the hills,*
> *And leaves a lonesome place against the sky.*

ACKNOWLEDGMENT

The foregoing papers, with one exception, first saw the light in the columns of *Reedy's Mirror,* the *Freeman,* the *Sewanee Review,* the *Open Court,* the *Mentor,* the *Double-Dealer* and *All's Well.* The exception is the essay on Ambrose Bierce, which was published in book form, in a limited edition, by Walter M. Hill of Chicago, who also published in attractive format the monograph on Arthur Machen, after its appearance in the *Mirror.* The paper on Stephen Crane, slightly abbreviated, was used as an introduction to a volume of Crane's stories, edited by me and published by Boni & Liveright.

To the editors of the several journals mentioned, to Mr. Hill, and to Boni & Liveright, Inc., I am grateful for cordial permission to reprint the various papers in the present volume. It should be added that all the essays have been revised and corrected, while a few have been rewritten; the long paper on Arthur Machen has been extended by more than twice its original material.

V. S.